B.J. Thomas &
Gloria Thomas

IN TUNE
Finding How Good Life Can Be

Fleming H. Revell Company
Old Tappan, New Jersey

Library of Congress Cataloging in Publication Data

Thomas, B.J.
        In Tune.

        1. Thomas, B.J. 2. Thomas, Gloria,
1949–   3. Converts—United States—
Biography.   4. Singers—United States—
Biography.   I. Thomas, Gloria, 1949–
II. Title.
BV4935.T45A34   1983   248'.0924   82–13327
ISBN 0–8007–1325–7

IN TUNE

Finding How Good Life Can Be

This book is dedicated to the following people for their loyalty and love, and for their willingness to lend their time, talents, and energy to a united cause:

Bev Mitchell
Joel Katz
Janet Kelly
Jim Manley
Diana Stagner
Freida Kudiabor

and the B.J. Thomas band: Jerry Thomas, Carl Greeson, Bobby Bain, Pat Vines, John Francis, Larry Chavis, Steve Hodge.

Contents

IN TUNE
Finding How Good Life Can Be

Raindrops or Storm Clouds?

I smiled at the desk clerk and continued walking across the lobby of the Biltmore Hotel in Los Angeles. I felt like Alice in Musicland, all dressed up and going to a gala occasion.

As we crossed the lobby and I saw bright sunlight streaming in, I realized it was only three in the afternoon. It seemed odd to be wearing evening clothes and having to wear sunglasses.

"Ready for the big event?" B.J. asked me. I could tell his mood was up in anticipation.

I smiled and nodded and gave his hand a squeeze.

It was February 27, 1980. We were on our way to the annual Grammy Awards at the Shrine Auditorium. B.J. had been nominated in the "Best Inspirational Performance" category.

"I hope you'll win again," I said for at least the fifth time that day. He had won the two previous years. We felt that the music B.J. was involved in now was some of the best he had ever done. And we hoped that his peers would agree.

The limo picked us up in front of our hotel and ten minutes later pulled up at the Shrine Auditorium. We saw, as in the previous years, the canopy and red carpet. Two men ran up to our limo and peered into the window, trying to identify any famous new arrivals.

"B.J. Thomas is here!" called out one of the men, as he waved to the TV camera already set up under the canopy.

We stepped out of the limousine and paused for only a second. I wore a dress of white hand-crocheted silk. A flush of excitement came over me. I glanced at B.J., and our eyes met in an unspoken message of love for each other. That look always reassured me more than words ever could.

B.J. had considered wearing a tux, but at the last minute he had bought a blue jacket of woven silk ribbon. He decided to wear that with his standard choice of pants: jeans.

Light almost blinded me as a camera swung our way, the hot lights adding to the ninety-degree temperature. The camera filmed every step as we walked down the red carpet.

People cheered and called out, "Go get 'em, B.J.!" I heard someone singing B.J.'s old standard, "Raindrops Keep Fallin' on My Head." I turned to see who was singing and smiled at him.

I was proud of my husband and proud to be with him. It excited me that fans recognized B.J. They cheered and shouted encouragement. And silently I thanked God for all of it.

As we approached the door, an announcer, mike in hand, grabbed B.J.'s other arm and pulled him aside. "Third year in a row for you, isn't it, Mr. Thomas? Do you think you'll win tonight? How does it feel to be nominated again?"

We'd heard all the questions before, and B.J. had given the answers time and again. But, in his usual way, B.J. smiled and answered as if this were the first time anyone had ever asked.

I stood aside, waiting until the questions were over, and the announcer said, "And another limousine has just pulled in . . ."

That was our cue. B.J. and I moved inside. The room—already half-filled with people running around shaking hands, hugging, and kissing—held a joyous kind of spirit about it.

Immediately we were caught up in the midst of the excitement. We saw other performers and leaders in the music business—people whose paths crossed only on special occasions such as the Grammy Awards.

"B.J.!"

I whirled around as Kenny Rogers grabbed me and hugged us

both. We chatted for several seconds before he moved on to greet someone else.

"You're both looking good," he turned and yelled back.

After the telecast, most of us went to the ground floor of the Biltmore for dinner and entertainment. Several top singers and groups would perform all evening in hour-long segments.

We took our reserved seats and waited for the pretelecast ceremony to begin. I knew that B.J.'s category was, as usual, near the bottom of the list, after jazz and the comedy album. The producer selected few of these for viewing on the home screen. But I didn't mind. B.J. had been nominated. I felt such pride in him.

From the corner of my eye, I looked at my husband. After ten years of marriage, I realized I loved him more now than I ever had before. It was almost as if B.J. and I had only discovered the real meaning of love in the past year.

Four years earlier both of us had begun a new stage in our lives. Up to then we had searched for meaning by trying all kinds of destructive ways. Now we had found answers. Now both of us were on the journey together.

Both of us had become born-again Christians. In early 1976 B.J. totally turned away from drugs and started his career all over. His being nominated for the Grammy Award became, for both of us, a symbol of a job well done. It proved that even though B.J.'s peers in the music business knew of his addiction and that he had overcome it, they still accepted him.

"Life has been getting better and better," I said, realizing that the two of us had come a long way together.

It wasn't over yet.

We had a long way to go before we had our lives fully in tune. Our turning to Jesus Christ had helped us begin to see that harmony was not only a possibility, it really *could* happen. We had gone through so much together. Now, daily and even painfully, we both determined to live in harmony with God and with each other. For the first time in our lives, B.J. and I were free. We loved life and had a reason to live.

Tears rushed to my eyes. We had come so far, and we had done it *together.*

My mind flashed back to the first time B.J. had been nominated for a Grammy Award—the highest, most visible award given to people in the music business. The nominations and the actual voting are done only by peers. B.J. had been nominated for the 1969 Grammy Award. We had been in Los Angeles that time, too. They presented the 1969 awards at the Century Plaza Hotel on March 11, 1970.

B.J. had been nominated for "Best Performance by a Male Vocalist" for the song "Raindrops Keep Fallin' on My Head." But he faced heavy competition: from Joe South for "Games People Play," Frank Sinatra for "My Way," Ray Stevens for "Guitarzan," and Harry Nilsson for "Everybody's Talkin'."

We really had expected B.J. to win. The "Raindrops" song had won him the respect he deserved. An earlier record, "Hooked on a Feeling," had sold more than a million copies. But "Raindrops" sold even better.

Still fairly unknown and new to the business, B.J. knew that winning would open new doors and push his career forward. I knew only that I wanted him to win. B.J. never said much. I didn't realize until years later how badly he had wanted to win.

Everything in his career happened so fast, and 1969 was the big year for him. That year he hit the top with his recording of the Burt Bacharach–Hal David song, "Raindrops." He had that big chance all singers yearn for.

Not that B.J. knew the song would hit the charts at the time. But the record pitched him into immediate fame. Ever since, people have always identified B.J. with that song.

From then on, life changed. People recognized him on the streets. Movie scripts came our way. TV talk-show hosts wanted interviews and personal appearances.

Had we been more seasoned, things might have gone differently. But we were two immature individuals when suddenly B.J. found himself in the limelight. The adulation proved too much for our already fragile lives.

On the one hand, success met us at every turn after "Raindrops." Yet that song also started the downward trend of our lives. I've often thought of that song not as raindrops, but as storm clouds over our heads.

2

Hooked on a Feeling

I flew to Los Angeles to meet B.J. when he was scheduled to record "Raindrops" for the sound track of the film *Butch Cassidy and the Sundance Kid*. He had already been on the road for nearly three weeks.

"Gloria!" he called and waved as he deplaned.

I shuddered when I saw him. He had that glassy look on his face which I had come to recognize as common among drug addicts. He had lost weight, too. I waved back.

He hugged me and said, "It's good to see you—"

"Your voice—your voice," I stammered.

"Just don't worry about it," he said and glared at me. "I guess it's a little raw."

"A little?"

I don't know how to describe my feelings. Both B.J. and I lived in a world of what counselors call dysfunctional thinking, and I couldn't have defined my emotions. Perhaps if I had been able to do that, we might have made progress much faster.

Looking back, I know guilt was always just below the surface. Sometimes guilt caused by what B.J. would say to me; other times by what he didn't say. I only know that in those days I felt unhappy and as though I had failed in my duties.

I didn't know until later that during that long tour he had hardly slept. He had been staying up all night, popping amphetamines, and staying high most of the time. B.J.'s addiction to prescription drugs should have been apparent to me all along. But I didn't recognize it as addiction. But then, I didn't want to, either.

He had begun to take pills openly at home. He was also taking them on his road trips—in even heavier doses. When he went through tense periods, or when trouble came, he increased the dosage. Sometimes he stayed awake for as long as three days.

That day, one of the executives from the studio talked to B.J. Realizing the seriousness of B.J.'s voice problem, he called Dionne Warwick's doctor. Within an hour after we checked into our hotel, the doctor had arrived.

After a lengthy examination, the doctor sighed. "The best medicine for you is silence. Don't talk for at least two weeks. You've irritated those vocal cords. Continued talking could do severe damage to them."

"I can't do that," B.J. said in a raspy voice. "I've got a recording session tomorrow." I quickly explained that B.J. had come to Los Angeles to sing the Burt Bacharach–Hal David song for a Robert Redford–Paul Newman movie called *Butch Cassidy and the Sundance Kid.*

"Man, I've *got* to do that recording," B.J. said.

"Do something," I begged.

"Well," the doctor said, "I can't perform magic, but I'll do what I can." He sprayed B.J.'s throat and then left, after giving us a handful of prescriptions.

The next day B.J. and I went to the studio. Because I knew him so well, I could sense the nervousness as he began. I tried not to let my face show the agony I went through as he sang in a scratchy voice.

When the recording session ended, a script supervisor grabbed B.J. and said, "What a marvelous interpretation! Just the way I imagine Paul Newman would sound."

B.J. smiled sheepishly, saying as little as possible, trying not to let everyone know he had no choice in how he sang.

The song was played in the film while Paul Newman, as Butch, rode Katherine Ross around on the handlebars of a bicycle.

We huddled together for a moment, chuckling. "I guess that man figured Butch Cassidy would sound like someone being choked."

"Maybe so," B.J. answered, outwardly treating the whole incident as though it was of little importance. I had not yet realized that when B.J. acted the most indifferent, he was most troubled.

Burt Bacharach, producer of the session, was justifiably furious however. He knew B.J.'s range and style. He got angry with B.J.'s manager for allowing him to strain his voice so badly.

Because of budget costs and fine-tune scheduling for this event, B.J. had no opportunity to rerecord. They had to go with the way he sang.

Although no one spoke to B.J. about his singing except the script supervisor, he knew himself that he had done a poor job. He did not need any put-down. He felt guilty enough.

As he left the studio, he swore and added, "I never liked that song much anyway."

I was to learn that that was another of B.J.'s defensive strategies. Because of his own insecurities, he covered his inadequacies by blaming others or by spewing out his anger.

By the time he recorded "Raindrops" again for the album, his voice had returned. The song hit the top of the charts immediately. "You've arrived," someone said to him. And we believed it. After that hit, almost everything B.J. recorded topped the charts.

"Everybody's Out of Town" followed the Bacharach–David song. Then a whole string of top-ten records such as "No Love At All," "Mighty Clouds of Joy," "Rock and Roll Lullaby," and "Just Can't Help Believing."

As success increased, however, our personal lives suffered. We drifted further apart. We saw it happening but were unable to change anything.

I kept thinking, *We'll adjust to this life-style,* and I tried not to give up hope. But I was only kidding myself.

I saw him becoming more and more dependent on amphetamines and Valium. *It's just nerves and pressure.* I had no idea how much more than that it was.

I suspected he was addicted, but I could not admit it, not even to myself. I covered for him, excused him, and found dozens of reasons

to ignore the mounting evidence. Or else I blamed myself. If I were
a better wife, I could help him more.

In those days almost everyone we knew in the business smoked
pot, at least. That extended beyond entertainers and included den-
tists, lawyers, even ophthamologists. Everybody had "a thing."

Frequently at parties someone would approach me and ask, "You
a vegetarian?"

"No," I'd reply.

"Smoke grass?"

The second question came as naturally as the first.

During those months immediately following "Raindrops" our
lives became horrible. Often I'd shut my eyes, wanting to blot it all
out. Almost wishing my husband had not burst onto center stage.

But as horrible as our lives became, I had no idea that the worst
was yet to come.

3

Running Scared

"B.J. has really screwed up his life," I said.

For a long time I had known he was an addict, and I used the word frequently. I just didn't want to face what that word involved.

Both of us were so young, and we didn't know how to cope. We didn't know anyone who had been into drugs and gotten free. Even if we had known someone like that, B.J. wouldn't have paid much attention. He knew he was hooked on drugs; but he could not yet admit that he couldn't kick them.

I knew only that he was miserable, and I was miserable. Because of his profession, we never had any kind of normal family life.

B.J. was already moving upward before we met in Houston in the fall of 1967. We married in December 1968, when "Eyes of a New York Woman" scored among the top ten. "Hooked on a Feeling" was on its way toward becoming B.J.'s second million-seller.

We had a wonderful future ahead—for both of us: B.J.'s career as a top recording artist, our new marriage, and then thirteen months later our daughter Paige was born. But those illusions of a wonderful future slowly crumbled. Aside from B.J.'s use of an increasing amount of drugs and the problems accompanying that, I had a difficult pregnancy, with bouts of depression. Then, after the birth, Paige herself changed the pattern of our lives, adding even more pressure.

Yet after Paige's birth, and during the troubled years that followed, we both acknowledged that Paige kept bringing us back together. Had it not been for the daughter we both loved, we would have divorced and gone our own ways. However, at the time of Paige's birth, we could only see her as one more pressure B.J. didn't need. And the pressures were mounting, priming B.J. to explode like a volcano.

He had been doing well, moving from local Texas singer to a recognized entertainer. In 1966 he released "I'm So Lonesome I Could Cry." It was his first million-seller. It put his name alongside the already famous.

Then came the pressures. Perhaps if we had known how the business operated, things might have been different. We could think only of recording a smash and putting B.J. at the top. Two gold records (each representing sales of one million copies) put him in a better position for getting a chance at the new songs.

Everything ought to have gone well for us. The money poured in. Yet, nothing went right. The more the money came in, the faster we spent it. The brighter B.J.'s star, the greater the pressures. "We'll have another big seller!" That was always the answer. "Just another big one," B.J. would say.

I'd agree. I wanted success and I wanted magic answers for the destructive problems facing us. Selling more records and bringing in higher grosses at concerts promised answers.

Even while the records sold and the tours brought in more money, little of it found its way into our pockets. Then came "Raindrops," the hit that would solve everything.

"Raindrops" was like the Trojan's wooden horse. It symbolized success, but it also helped bring about our destruction.

We were still blaming everything and everybody for our problems. One of our favorite scapegoats was New York City. We lived in Memphis after we married, and then nine months later, in the fall of 1969, we moved to Manhattan.

The problems multiplied. B.J. seemed to double his drug intake. He had been on drugs of some kind since he was fifteen. But only after living in New York did he start to accept the fact that the drugs controlled him.

The horror began. B.J. would perform his gigs. Afterward, he'd still be so high that he would disappear for hours. Sometimes he'd whizz through New York in a rented Lincoln, hitting fenders and smashing cars. On one occasion he brought home our Cadillac (one of the four cars we owned at that time) with at least eight colors of paint on the smashed fenders.

"What happened?"

"Nobody messes with me," he said, brushing past me. I never knew how he would react. Often he'd be irrational, as in this instance. At other times he would be so funny that I would laugh with him.

He went into the bedroom and collapsed. He slept until an hour before show time.

"B.J., honey, you need help," I said to him after he woke up. I had already said those words several times.

"I don't need help. I can lick this myself," he'd say.

"But you're not—"

"Get off my back and leave me alone!"

We argued back and forth for weeks. I'd try every kind of approach I knew. "Hey, B.J., you can go someplace and dry out. It won't be for long, and you'll be able to continue—"

"I don't need a doctor," he'd say and swear at me.

"But you do—"

"No doctor can help. I'm taking these drugs for a reason," he'd say in his most macho voice. "When that reason's gone, I'll quit." But B.J. never explained the reason. I don't think he knew what it was himself.

But I kept pleading.

Others urged him to get help.

One day B.J. announced we were moving to the country. "Get out of this sewer," he said. "Then I can straighten out."

I wanted to believe him. Besides, I was desperate enough to grab at any answer.

We found a beautiful, stone country house in Connecticut. I thought of it as the kind of house Prince Charming and Cinderella would have lived in. We purchased the house, which included four and a half acres of landscaped lawn and a fifty-foot pool. The eighty-year-old house was like a stone fortress with thick, double hardwood doors. A stone wall encircled the entire property. The two-block-long driveway ended in a parking area with a cabana and basketball court.

We paid more than we should have, and the house required expensive maintenance. But in those days we didn't think much about money. We were escaping from the city and from B.J.'s pressures.

We lived in the house, holding the world and its problems at bay. Unfortunately, the problems within the walls intensified. We discovered that our fortress had been penetrated and our illusion of security sabotaged. Finally even B.J. admitted that merely leaving New York didn't solve our problems.

B.J.'s drug escapades got worse. We were so desperate, so unhappy, and in so much pain. "There has to be a way not to hurt so much," I finally said.

At that moment I looked into B.J.'s eyes. They were like silver blue tombstones. I had never seen as much sadness in anyone's eyes as I saw in my husband's that day.

He had to get help. I couldn't let our pain continue to overwhelm us.

"Please," I said for at least the tenth time that day. I had argued and cajoled, given B.J. the silent treatment, stormed out of the room and slammed the door behind me. I had tried everything I knew. This time I pleaded. "Please, not only for yourself, but for me. For Paige."

I don't know if I weakened him with my persistence or if it was because I mentioned our young daughter, but B.J. relented.

He nodded his head. "You set up the appointment and I'll go."

As I picked up the phone, I looked once again at those lackluster eyes. The sadness in them almost made me lose my composure as I dialed the phone. One of our friends had given me the name of a psychiatrist. I set up the appointment.

For the first few weeks I felt as if the cavalry had just ridden across the horizon, trumpets blowing, ready to battle the evil elements threatening to destroy us. We had finally found some help.

For more than a year B.J. went to his doctor. As the weeks wore on, I saw no change. He certainly took pills as heavily as before.

Finally I talked to the doctor myself. "But he's no better," I said. Often I would break down and cry. My cavalry had been another illusion.

The times I saw the doctor, I usually ended up with a prescription for tranquilizers and a kind admonition to be patient.

I had difficulty getting straight answers from the doctor. He never actually said these words, but I felt he was telling me, "If B.J. can accept his anxieties as being normal for him, he can adjust better to the world around him."

But B.J. didn't adjust. He got worse. And each time he would call the psychiatrist for help. At least three times the doctor and lawyers bailed B.J. out of jail. On one occasion, still high after finishing up an evening in a New York supper club, he went out on the streets, wrecked his car, and beat up a pedestrian. It took nine policemen to subdue him.

They took B.J. to jail again. By then, the psychiatrist had fallen into the same pattern as so many others—yielding to B.J. in illogical ways because of who he was. B.J. had only to call and the psychiatrist would run to him. No matter whether day or night, he would drop everything else for his famous patient.

That night the psychiatrist called to tell me that B.J. was back in jail. I had already gone through so many drug episodes and midnight phone calls I was exhausted. I felt so tired I could hardly talk.

"I can't have him home," I said. "If he comes home I'll have to come up with so much energy that I don't have. And I can't stop it from happening again. I—I just can't take it again."

"We'll transfer him to a private drug-treatment center in Westport," the doctor said, "but we need your signed permission."

"I want him to stay until he gets the drugs out of his system," I said.

"I won't be responsible for what might happen to him," the doctor said, "if he stays in that jail."

"But will he stay long enough at Westport to do any good?"

"We'll take care of him, Gloria. All we need is your signature."

The doctor won again. He always won because he knew what to

say and how to manipulate me. If I didn't sign, B.J. wouldn't get help at the treatment center. If I did sign, I knew the doctor would have him out again in a few days.

Underneath it all, guilt stirred. I couldn't have defined it so easily then, but I felt I had failed my husband. If only I had been more supportive. Or maybe more aggressive in challenging his drug habit. But no matter what choices I made, they were always the wrong ones.

A few days after entering the private hospital, B.J. came home to his stash of drugs. "Let's not worry," he said. "We'll get through this."

The army of people around B.J.—from agents to business managers—protected him by bailing him out of one jam after another. As each horror unfolded, ending with the inevitable payoff, I kept hoping it would be the last time. But it never was. His protectors kept B.J. from experiencing natural cause-and-effect results from the choices he made.

I realize now that the psychiatrist was the worst one of all. He was so busy star kissing, he did nothing to help.

The horror scenes occurred with greater frequency and intensity. It was not just the arrests and his entourage hiding it from the public, financial collapse was threatening. Bills did not get paid. We overdrew our credit card limit. The dynasty was starting to crumble, and we felt helpless.

While we felt that many of our employees were not acting in B.J.'s best interests, we could do nothing. He couldn't cope with his professional life, because our homelife was in a shambles. And B.J.'s drug habit was costing him between two and three thousand dollars a week.

Somehow we also ended up supporting B.J.'s relatives—many of whom had drug habits of their own. After a while it seemed as if all we had to do was talk to someone and before long we were paying that person's rent, too.

B.J. began working less. The lawyer and the business manager constantly urged me, "Gloria, you've got to help him make this engagement."

"But he can't—"

"He's got to."

"He's sick."

"He's been sick before."

I'd give in and endure another argument with B.J. In the end, B.J. would agree to perform. Sometimes he would leave home for a show and never appear. At other times, he arrived, but never walked on stage. Because he broke contracts for appearances, the lawsuits piled up.

This not only meant loss of income, B.J. also began to acquire a bad reputation—he was no longer dependable, so he constituted a high risk.

Life started closing in on us. I was frightened, not knowing what to do. But even in my immaturity, I knew I would survive. *I'll find an answer,* I kept telling myself. I had always found a way in the past. My childhood had ingrained in me that pattern of assuming responsibility and finding solutions.

"We can't go on like this," I said to B.J. on one of those occasions when we talked without arguing.

"What can we do about it?" he asked.

"I don't know. But we'll do something. We're going to break out of this."

At my insistence we stopped seeing the psychiatrist. Not only was he not helping B.J., I felt he had actually made things worse. I had nothing better to suggest, but I felt *I* had to find the answer.

I had been trained, unconsciously, to feel that as long as B.J. had a problem, I had an obligation. It became my problem, too. In a totally illogical way, I felt responsible for his failures as though I had caused them or could cure them.

"We'll find a way. We'll get help," I promised over and over.

We were both miserable together. Yet for such a long time neither of us could think about leaving the other. We both came from emotionally deprived backgrounds, where no one freely expressed love. Both of us needed to be loved, and we searched for that special love from each other.

No matter how angry or confused I became, I knew I loved B.J. And I knew he loved me. We had that much going for us all along, even during the worst scenes. The moment I met B.J. I fell in love with him. He had exactly the same response to me. From that moment on, we felt bound to each other. And that bond wasn't always pleasant. We vacillated from being drunk with love to inflicting hate and scorn on each other. But, for good or bad, neither of us had another day without the other occupying much of our thoughts. And we stayed together.

But the day came when I could no longer cope. Even though I loved B.J., I had often thought of leaving him. After six years of marriage, I finally made the break.

I packed clothes for Paige and myself and moved to Fort Worth, Texas, as far away from B.J. and the New York scene as I could get.

I left, wondering and worrying all the time. B.J. had been the center of my life. Could I survive without him? Then I turned the question around and asked, *Could I survive if I stayed?* Even after I left, it took me five months to find rest from the anguish that our life together had given me. I grieved every day, but I did survive.

We stayed apart eight months. But even apart, we both knew torment. The difference now was that we knew our torment separately.

During the last two months of separation, I constantly fought depression. I found relief only when B.J. came through Fort Worth.

"How you doing?" he'd always ask.

"I miss you and I'm miserable," and I'd cry. I did not want to cry and tried to hold back the tears, but they came anyway.

"I miss you, too," he said, and the tone of his voice let me know how miserable he felt.

We missed each other so much, we forgot how hard it had been to live together. Our quick contacts—usually lasting a day or two at most—wiped from our memories the pain we had shared for six years. Apart, we both suffered from loneliness and grief.

Finally B.J. said, "Will you come back, Gloria?"

"Yes," I said without hesitating, and the merry-go-round started up again.

B.J. had lived on the road most of the time since I left Connecticut. He left the house himself soon afterward and never went back. When we reunited, we sold our country home.

We had solved nothing in our eight months of separation. The year we stayed together afterward was even more difficult than the previous years. We were running—and running scared. Details of that year remain sketchy in my memory. I know that I hardly functioned.

I felt that some of our staff patronized me—not so much in actual words, but in their attitudes. "Just take care of B.J.," they'd say.

I can take partial blame for our lack of establishing a good relationship. I was suspicious of everyone, held myself back, and was hard to get to know.

When B.J. would get sick, unable to function, they'd call me for help.

"Gloria, he's got to perform. You've got to make him."

"But he can't," I would protest. "He could kill himself."

"We can't take another lawsuit," they'd say.

No matter what I said, or how I tried to explain, they made me feel guilty if I didn't push B.J. to perform. Over a period of months I realized they didn't care about him. He was a product. They felt satisfied as long as he made one more performance, one more guest shot, cut one more album. B.J. was killing himself, but they didn't seem to notice. Or care.

Surprisingly, no matter how sick or how crazy B.J. got from his drug taking, he could always sing.

In April 1975, his version of "Hey, Won't You Play Another Somebody Done Somebody Wrong Song?" reached number one on the charts and became a million-seller.

Until that point, I had always been involved in every project, watching it take shape. I was there when the project was born and followed its rise and fall on the charts. But this time I didn't involve myself. I didn't care. I was so miserable again I could hardly survive. I spent my time in a daze, just enduring until the night. At night I couldn't sleep and often sat staring into darkness, waiting for the dawn.

The day B.J. went to the studio in Nashville to record the follow-up to "Wrong Song" I left. Paige and I flew back to a rented house in Fort Worth.

B.J. didn't come back to Fort Worth. Instead he flew to Los

Angeles and leased a house there. Both of us left—both of us still trying to run away. We could no longer stand the misery we inflicted on each other when we were together.

I left Nashville, wishing I had someone to go to. I determined never to go back to the drug-crazed world again.

A woman I had known, Faye, took care of Paige most of the time. I knew my daughter needed someone, but I couldn't function. I got up every morning, walked trancelike through the day, and seemed unable to think about even the basics such as washing clothes or preparing meals.

I started having fainting spells. One time when I fainted somebody (I assume Faye) called a doctor. I woke up in the hospital. I have no recollection of what happened.

Later, the police suspected I may have intercepted robbers.

"But I didn't see anyone," I said, my brain still foggy.

The starter on my car had given me trouble, so I had it towed away for repairs. Then someone stole our dog. Robbers, seeing no car, may have assumed no one was home. "Sounds like the common pattern, ma'am," the policeman said. "No car. No animal to warn them."

I remembered only that I had slid open the glass door which led to the patio. Later, I half-crawled from the patio into the living room. Faye found a pool of blood where I must have lain for some time on the patio.

I stayed in the hospital nine days. They called it exhaustion. No exaggeration there. Even when I came home, I felt as though my senses were still drugged. The back of my head was so bad that most of the time in the hospital, they had tubes connected to drain out the fluid.

For a full two months after my fall—or attack—my memory played tricks on me. I couldn't remember simple things, or I'd forget the name of a family member. I'd walk into the kitchen for something and then stand in the middle of the room for ten minutes trying to remember what it was.

The situation with B.J. didn't improve. He would call on the phone, either very high or extremely low. He'd promise money and then not send it. Or I would receive only part of what he promised.

My bills mounted up, and I had no way to pay them.

"I can't take any more," I cried out, "I can't take any more."

But I did. His phone calls became even more erratic. Bill collectors called. I hated to open the mail because someone was always threatening to sue me for nonpayment.

I even tried prayer. Some days I pleaded, "God, get me out of this mess."

At times I'd lash out at God, "I don't even know if You're real. If You are, help me!"

Or I'd bargain, "If You'll just get me through all this, I'll do anything You want. I promise, God."

It didn't matter how I prayed. My own words mocked me. I was getting no better, and life was closing in on me. Thoughts of suicide came often. Had I not been responsible for Paige, I probably would have killed myself. Other than the love I felt for my daughter and the empty ache for B.J., I had nothing left—nothing to live for.

And then, at my darkest hour, God answered me through a strange phone call.

4

Finding the Light

The phone rang. I picked it up.

"Mrs. Thomas? Mrs. Gloria Thomas?"

"Yes."

"The wife of B.J. Thomas?" the man's voice asked.

"Yes," I said. B.J. and I had been separated three weeks, and I had no intention of ever getting back with him again, but I had told no one of my plans.

Once the strange voice knew who I was, he said, "I'm calling to talk to you about investing some of your excess capital."

Slowly the words penetrated. *"Excess capital?"* I shrieked.

As if I could no longer control myself, the words flew. "You want to know about my excess capital? B.J. and I split up three weeks ago. I have no idea where he is now. His manager stopped sending me money, and I'm twenty-five hundred dollars overdrawn at the bank. I have all kinds of stores threatening to sue me. I may end up in jail and lose my child. Right now I don't even have food in the house!"

I wasn't finished. The story had even more details. In a fit of anger, B.J. had stolen my car in the middle of the night after visiting me. I had no transportation. My younger sister had died tragically in Houston. A friend from Nashville told me that B.J. was living with some Playboy Bunny in Los Angeles.

"I was hospitalized for eight days, separated from my daughter! I have no idea how I'm going to pay those bills!"

I paused for breath.

"I'm sorry, Mrs. Thomas—"

"Sorry? And you know how I survived the past week since getting out of the hospital? I had a garage sale. So, mister, if you can find surplus capital, you're welcome to take all of it and invest it anyplace you like!"

When I finished my tirade he introduced himself and said, "I'm Micah Reeves' brother-in-law."

Micah Reeves. I had met her months earlier. She was about my age—perhaps twenty-five or twenty-six, dark, with loose-fitting clothes. I remembered her as a pleasant woman who spoke in a kind of gruff voice.

"May I tell Micah about your situation?" he asked.

"Mister, you can tell Micah. You can tell the president. You can tell . . ." I must have babbled on, and finally the telephone conversation ended. I had scarcely hung up when the phone rang again.

"This is Micah," she said.

She asked questions, and I poured out my story again, this time in a more subdued manner. Not that I wanted to tell everyone my problems, but I had been alone so long and no one had cared.

"I'll be right over," she said and got my address. "Anything else I can bring besides food?"

I could think only of the piles of dirty clothes. I didn't even know how to use the washing machine. I hadn't been able to function enough to try. "Just—just a box of Tide so I can wash Paige's clothes."

Within an hour, Micah arrived and took charge. She cooked and then sat down across from me to make sure both Paige and I ate. She heard the whole story again while the automatic washer scrubbed our clothes.

At one point I asked myself, *Why am I telling her all this? Micah and I are so different.* I had experienced more of the world and this naive, conservative Texan, who found a word like *damn* blasphemous, sat across from me.

I couldn't answer my question except I knew one thing: Micah genuinely cared.

Just before leaving, she laid her car keys on the table. "Here. I'm leaving this for as long as you need the car."

I stared at her. "Your car? I can't—"

"Yes you can," she said in that characteristic gruff way.

"But—but I don't want your car."

"That's God's car," she said.

"But I might wreck it, or—"

"If God wants the car wrecked, then you might as well do it." She wouldn't take no for an answer. Her husband, Jim, came by to pick her up and they left.

I began seeing a lot of Micah and Jim. They became my only friends. While they were as different from me as anyone I'd ever met in my life, they kept coming.

And they talked about God.

During those long hours with them I asked seventeen thousand questions. They always answered, and I kept asking. I was careful to give no indication that I believed anything they said. I just kept asking. Some of my questions made them uncomfortable. At times I felt they wanted to say, "Shut up, Gloria." But they never did.

Micah patiently listened, answered, and would often add, "If you'll just turn your life over to Jesus Christ, Gloria, everything will work out."

Then we didn't see each other for several weeks. My brother Tracy had come to live with me, and we moved to a rented apartment in Arlington, Texas.

Other than giving Paige the minimum care, I stayed inside the apartment, mostly in the bedroom. I lived on raw fruits and nuts, because I couldn't cook or do anything that took serious concentration. I couldn't even plan a meal or a trip to the grocer's.

One day I picked up a record that B.J. had recorded in 1975. One cut was called "Bally-Hoo Days." I listened.

> Sitting by the stage door of the Palace;
> Looking down the alley two ways.
> One way takes my mind back home to Alice,
> The other to my Bally-hoo days.

There was a time my name had swept the nation,
Now my job is sweeping cafes.
I wonder how much living I have wasted,
Clinging to my Bally-hoo days.

Bally-hoo days, Bally-hoo days.
God Almighty, when I go,
Please let me go dancing, dancing.
I've seen life from both sides of the curtain,
But the only life for me is the stage.
And nowadays, my work is more uncertain,
And filled with dreams of Bally-hoo days.

Bally-hoo days, Bally-hoo days.
God Almighty, when I go,
Please let me go dancing, dancing
in a Bally-hoo way,
Like my Bally-hoo days.

I listened to that cut over and over. I started to cry. "That's B.J.'s life—he's singing his own story," I sobbed. "That's the only reality he knows—performing."

I got up and looked at myself in the mirror. My hollow cheeks and lackluster eyes made me look twice my age. My appearance was no lie, I felt that bad—or worse.

What am I going to do?

I was down to my last few dimes. I had no prospects for work and no training. The best I could hope for was a menial job at minimum wage. But even at that moment, I worried more about B.J. than I did about Paige and me. At least I had Micah and Jim. He had no one.

Micah and I began seeing each other again. As before, she kept telling me about a loving God. "He'll meet you wherever you are, Gloria."

"Yeah? He hasn't done anything yet."

"He's waiting for you to surrender to Him."

"He'll perform miracles in your life," Jim echoed.

I had heard it over and over. I also watched that couple. Their words told me nothing that I hadn't heard since childhood. But their lives began getting through to me. They had no reason to befriend me. *Especially* someone like me—so different from them, with a totally different life-style and set of values. Yet they cared. That touched me more than the seven billion words they spoke over the months.

A few days before Christmas, Paige and I spent the evening at the Reeves' house. I knew something would have to happen soon. I was beginning to pull out of my depression. I still worried constantly about B.J.—especially when it would be a full week between phone calls.

"Something's got to happen soon," I said to my friends.

As we left their house, Micah said, "We're praying for you." But she had said that a hundred times before.

"Our church prays for you, too," Jim reminded me.

I hugged them both, thanked them, and got into the car. I started driving home. It was late, and six-year-old Paige lay down in the backseat and fell asleep almost immediately.

Suddenly a pain struck me in the chest. Not an actual physical sensation, yet so strong I gasped. Those thousands of questions I had asked now filled my head. The questions and the Reeves' answers to them blocked out everything else. My head spun, and I drove mechanically the rest of the way home. As soon as I got there, I hurriedly put Paige to bed.

I went to my room. But I knew I couldn't sleep. I also knew that I couldn't run anymore. I had reached the end. If there was any answer for me, it had to be found in Jesus Christ. The Reeves' message had finally penetrated.

"God, please—please help me," I sobbed.

I don't know how long I prayed or what I said, but I know that everything changed. Instead of the torment that had pervaded the room, a spirit of peace now filled every corner.

I knelt beside the bed and, between my tears, I thanked God. "I give myself to You, God. This time without any reservation I turn myself over to You."

In the minutes that followed, I surrendered everything to Him: Paige, B.J., our marriage, my future.

When I paused and raised my head, I knew I was different. I could not explain what had happened to me. I felt the entire world fall from my shoulders. I was a new person.

I could hardly wait to call the Reeves. They shouted and wept and prayed with me on the phone. The next morning, even little Paige seemed to understand. During all my times of torment, she had been attending a Christian school. She, in her simple way, knew more about Jesus Christ than I did.

There was still one more person I wanted to tell.

5

Born Again

A few days later B.J. called. "How're you doing?"

"I'm doing fine. Just fine." My own answer surprised me. Usually our conversations started with an angry answer from me, which set the stage for the rest of the conversation. I always yelled at him for not sending us enough money. I pushed every guilt button I could, reminding him of his neglect of Paige.

I always tried to talk him into searching for a new approach. "There has to be a way," I often said. Since I believed I had to search until I found the right way, I pushed him, too. I had depended upon my words and urgings to change B.J. Now I knew it would take something more.

The conversation limped along, neither of us raising our voices.

"You sound different," he said.

"I feel different."

"What's going on?"

I took a quick breath and closed my eyes. This was the opportunity I had been waiting for. *Please, Lord. Please help me.* I, who always had solutions to problems, did not know what to say. Now that I had come to know the God who is a Spirit, my words seemed inadequate. At the same time, I had a marvelous sense of knowing God could reach B.J. "Paige and I—we have both become born-again Christians."

"Oh," he said.

His noncommittal answer made me want to plead with him to turn to God, too. But then, both of us had come from religiously conservative backgrounds. Both of us had accepted the Lord a thousand times since childhood, so the term *born again* did not mean much.

"I've changed, B.J."

"Yeah," he said, and I could detect no emotion in his voice.

"B.J., come home. I've found help. There's help for you, too."

"I don't know—I don't know if I can or not . . ." his voice trailed off.

"Okay," I said, for once not pressing him. "Whenever you can make it."

"I'll come for a visit."

"Fine," I said.

"Right after Christmas."

"Okay."

"I'd like to be there."

"Well, if you decide to come home, there's help for you here."

B.J. had run from trouble all his life. Even his pills helped him retreat from facing reality. He hung up without promising to come home.

As I put the phone down, I felt we had reached another impasse. That's how our conversations always ended. Most of them involved screaming and swearing and sometimes his incoherent babbling. But always at an impasse.

But this time one thing had been different—*me.*

I felt peace. I had spoken with a calmness I had never experienced before. My heart ached for B.J., yet I didn't scream, cajole, or plead.

Later B.J. said, "You were different. I could tell."

"How?" I asked, wondering what specifically I had said.

"Not the words, Gloria. But *you*—you were different."

I smiled. So typical of B.J. He's a rare and sensitive person. He walks into a room and senses people's attitudes. Even over the phone, he knew I had changed, but he was not willing to admit it then or to acknowledge the cause of my change.

After hanging up, I prayed again for my husband. I didn't have a hundred nagging ideas for B.J. this time as I always did when he called.

"Jesus, I know what You did for me. I know You can do it for him." And for the first time in years, I felt hope for B.J.

During the days that followed I wavered between hope and despair for B.J. I sincerely believed that if he came back home, Jesus Christ would change him. But I sensed that time was running out for him. His body couldn't take the drugs forever. I felt he was coming to some kind of a final crossroads in life. I sensed resignation in his voice.

Later B.J. was to tell me he had the same premonition. He had given up the will to live. He moved from one day to the next, not caring if he survived or not.

For the first time I knew the sound of inner harmony because of Christ's coming into my life.

B.J. began sending money again, although seldom the amount he had promised. Before my conversion, when I asked for more, he'd swear and scream at me. "You think that's all I've got to do? Bust myself on that stage so I can send you money?"

"You owe it to us!"

"I owe you? After all you've done to me?" (He seldom said exactly what I had done, other than walk out on him.)

Or I'd take the aggressive role. "You have a daughter, you know! She's here in this world because of you as much as because of me!"

"And you never let me forget it for one minute, do you?"

"How can I forget it? I have to live here with her and look at her lack of clothes. We can't go anyplace or do anything because you won't send enough money . . ."

After a while we probably could have repeated the dialogue in our sleep. Except we kept saying it on the phone.

Looking back, I realize that he did send me enough to live on, had I only known how to be practical. But I had no sense of practicality. Until Jesus Christ began changing my life, I never stopped to reason out the consequences of decisions. I spent money without thinking of the next day, let alone the next week.

When we had moved to Arlington, I had hired a young black woman to help. She brought a friend named Beverly Mitchell. Beverly and I developed an immediate rapport. Before she left she gave me her telephone number and said, "If you ever need me, just call."

Need her? I sure needed *somebody.* Somebody to take care of me. Somebody to help me cope.

"Oh, I do need you," I said. She came back the next day.

Bev came frequently. She cleaned the house and she guided me through the day. I didn't have the money to spend for her services, but she was as necessary to my survival as food. I honestly believe that if I had had to choose between food or paying her wages, I would still have called Bev.

I had just taken the horrible bandages off my head. My memory was still not normal. My head ached constantly. Bev took care of Paige and the house. Most of all, she took care of me.

Bev sat, often for hours, listening to me pour out my soul. She never let me get too low because she'd flash a smile at me or say something funny. Soon I'd laugh. On the days when Bev came, I felt better. I began to know I would survive this, too.

She took Paige to and from school. She washed clothes and cared for Paige. Most of all, she loved my daughter, and Paige responded to her.

Most of the time I prayed and read my Bible.

"God, please, get hold of B.J." I must have asked for that six million times. And inside I knew that if he was ever to follow Jesus Christ, he must make his decision soon.

"He needs You so much, Lord."

6

A Child's Faith

I looked at the calendar. But I already knew what day it was— *January 26.* During a second phone call after my conversion, B.J. had promised that he would come to see us on January 26. As I lay in bed, fully awake, I prayed that he would.

He's made so many promises he hasn't kept—

No! I stopped. I wouldn't allow myself to think those negative thoughts. B.J. had promised to come. I kept praying.

Later, I went into the kitchen. Paige was already up, dressed, and eating a bowl of cereal. She looked up at me, "Mama, I have a wonderful surprise for you."

"What's that?"

"Bandit. He likes me now."

I could hardly believe it. Bandit, a white Lhasa apso, jumped up on her lap and licked her face. Paige crinkled her nose and laughed. "See? See? Bandit does love me."

I shook my head in amazement. Neighbors had given Bandit to us before they moved. I had hesitated to accept a dog, but then I reasoned Paige might not feel so lonely with a dog around. But Bandit didn't like children. He followed me around. He would sit on my lap or get playful around me but would have nothing to do with my daughter.

Yet, as I stood in the kitchen, Paige and Bandit played with each other. She'd toss him a biscuit, and he'd bark, jump for it, and come back for more.

"Oh, Paige, Bandit loves you. He really does!"

"I know that, Mama," she said matter-of-factly. "That's what I prayed for." She stopped and took several bites of cereal.

"You prayed—"

"That's right. At school, we have church, you know, and our teacher said that we should pray for things we want. So I prayed for Bandit to love me."

"Oh, darling," I said and hugged her. Tears sprang to my eyes as I listened to her simple story. She had prayed, believed, and had been delightfully happy at the change in Bandit, but she was not surprised.

"Know what else I prayed for, Mommy?"

"No, what?"

"For Daddy. That he would come home today."

I hugged her again, not trusting my voice to answer. I wanted to tell her that he was coming home today. *But was he?* I didn't have the heart to get her hopes up and then have them destroyed if he failed to show up. "Let's wait and see," I said.

"Oh, he's coming all right. I know he is."

After she had gone to school, the phone rang. It was B.J.

He called from the airport in Los Angeles. "I'm not going to make the flight, Gloria."

"Oh?" I said, wanting to lash out at him, but I held back. "I—I wish you would come. It's especially important to Paige." I was surprised how calm my voice sounded even to me.

"Why?"

I told him about Bandit, and then I said, "She asked God for something else. She asked Him to send you home today."

For a long moment B.J. did not answer. I could hear the background noise of the airport. "Let me hang up, Gloria. I'm going to try to get myself together and come home."

He told me his arrival time. I drove to the airport to meet the plane, still not knowing whether he would be on it or not. I wanted him to come, but I was scared.

The last time we had been together he had gone on a rampage. He struck me, screamed at me for over an hour, and stormed out of the house. When he was on drugs, there was no telling what kind of mood I'd find him in.

He deplaned with the first-class passengers. When our eyes met, the moment was awkward. He smiled once more as he moved toward me.

I stared at him, trying to figure out his mood. His dark hair, always curly, seemed more so, as though he had rumpled it with a towel and let it dry that way. *I like it that way,* I said to myself. His face had that emaciated look, like skin stretched over bone. I guessed there were only about 130 pounds on that six-foot frame. And I knew how much I still loved him.

We grabbed each other. He kissed me quickly and hugged me again. "How are you?" he asked.

"I'm all right."

"You look fine," he said, quickly surveying me.

I didn't know if I looked fine or not, but it didn't matter.

"How's the weather?"

"All right. Not as cold as you'd expect . . . "

"Any rain?"

"No."

As we left the airport and started home, our inane conversation continued. After all, we had been living apart for almost a year. We had so much to catch up on, yet both of us were afraid to jump in too quickly.

I remember little of the drive home. He sat beside me, continuing with the small talk. Both of us guarded each word, neither wanting to open the wound first. Both afraid the other might start the attack.

When Paige came home from school, she squealed in ecstasy. "I knew you'd be here! I knew you would! I told everyone at school you were coming home today!"

B.J. grabbed her, swung her in the air, and then kissed her. For the rest of that day, Paige became the focus of our attention. Both of us were too scared to focus on anything else.

I had been talking to B.J. about what had happened to me and about Micah and Jim's influence. "This time it's real, B.J. I know I'm different."

He didn't say much, mostly he listened. I'd think he was going to ask for help, and then he'd get up and go to the fridge for a drink. But he didn't argue with me. Although he said little, he did listen.

A couple of days later at about five o'clock in the afternoon I said, "Paige and I are going over to Micah's. She needs her steamer pot back. Want to come along?"

"Over there? I don't want to go."

"Why not?"

"They are the people who helped you and I'm glad for that, but I don't want to talk to them."

"Look, we won't stay more than ten minutes. I promise. I'd just like you to meet them."

"Come on, Daddy, please," Paige begged.

"I don't know—"

"Look, I have to go. I promised. You can see I'm not planning to stay." I was wearing no makeup. I had on a long dress that I only wore around the house. My hair needed setting. "I promised to return the steamer. That's all I'm going to do."

B.J. followed us to the car, saying nothing. When we arrived at Micah's house he said, "I'll sit and wait here."

"Oh, come on. I'd like you to meet them."

"Okay, then we'll go out and get a hamburger or something. Okay?"

"Great, Daddy," Paige said and jumped out of the car.

We rang the bell, and Micah appeared almost immediately. I handed her the pot, introduced B.J., and said, "We just came by long enough to return this—"

"I'm just getting supper. It's almost ready. Don't you want to stay and eat with us?" she asked.

I looked at B.J. and was already set to explain that we didn't have time. "Well, I guess we can stay a little," B.J. said.

"Oh, good," she said. And we went in.

While we waited for Micah to finish cooking supper, B.J. and I watched the children play. Then B.J. turned on the TV for the news. He didn't say much, but then unless he is in a talkative mood, B.J. is a rather quiet person anyway.

Later he told me he sensed that he had stepped into a loving home. The children played together in a way he had never seen children act before. Whatever that family had, we didn't. He also sensed that, if he stayed, he could get help.

"Jim won't be home until late. He's working the rodeo in Fort Worth."

"Oh," he said.

"I wish you could meet him," Micah added. "Probably won't be in until ten-thirty or so, though."

B.J. never said he would wait. He stared at the TV. My eyes focused on the set, but inwardly I was praying. *Lord, make him stay until Jim gets home. If only he'll stay, I know Jim will help him.*

We finished supper. Micah and I washed dishes, cleared the kitchen, and talked about the Lord all the time.

"If you want to stay, Jim will be coming home—I'd like to have you meet him," Micah said about seven-thirty.

"Don't want to stay too long," B.J. answered. I expected him to get up any minute, stretch, and say, "Let's go." But he didn't.

Micah sat down across from B.J. She told him about her own experience with Jesus Christ.

Jim finally walked in. He greeted B.J., and we made small talk for a few minutes. Then he smiled. "Jesus Christ has already made a difference in Gloria's life."

"I know He has."

"He can do the same for you."

B.J. only nodded slightly. It has always been hard for me to know what's going on in his head when he acts that way. I know he's in deep thought, but his face gives no indication of how he's responding.

"Why don't you just give Jesus Christ a chance?" Jim said that several times.

Each time B.J. only listened, saying nothing.

After about twenty minutes Jim said, "Let's you and me go into the den where we can talk alone."

B.J. shrugged and followed Jim.

They stayed in there a long time. We couldn't hear anything they said, but Micah and I both prayed silently.

Then I heard B.J.'s voice. He was praying, following Jim's prompting, "O God, be merciful to me, a sinner."

Micah and I raced into the room. Micah hugged me when we saw the scene before us: Both men were kneeling, B.J.'s head was bowed, and Jim's arm was around him.

Just as B.J. raised his head, the grandfather clock struck midnight, January 28, 1976.

Five years later, as I sat next to B.J. in that Shrine Auditorium, pieces of those years flashed through my mind. We had come so far together. We were discovering what being in tune really meant. Not being in tune just with each other but also in tune with God. We were beginning to know how good life could really be.

Hearing the announcement of B.J.'s category jarred my thoughts back into the present. The announcer read the list of nominees for the best inspirational performance by a male artist.

I tensed, waiting for him to announce the winner. And in that split second, I remembered vividly the first experience when B.J. had been nominated for "Raindrops."

That night the announcer had said, "And the winner is—Harry Nilsson for 'Everybody's Talkin'.' "

After losing the award, B.J. had to go on before that crowd of performers and sing. And he did. Even though he was brokenhearted, his performance never showed his pain.

Now our lives were different. Even though we wanted to win, our security wasn't based on winning or losing. Now we had Jesus Christ to strengthen us in our disappointments.

"And the winner is—B.J. Thomas!"

"Thanks, Lord," I said aloud, tears filling my eyes. I was so thankful to God and so proud of B.J.

As B.J. went forward to receive his Grammy Award, I thanked God again for showing us that He was pleased with our lives. That award symbolized His blessings as well as the acceptance of B.J. by his peers in the music business.

7

The "Emergency Room Church"

The way we felt for the first months following B.J.'s conversion was the closest we had come to experiencing flying among the clouds—like Peter Pan, the two of us. Being born again does bring with it a childlike magic. The experience develops and changes but never goes away. We learned that even in the midst of the most devastating circumstances our relationship with God kept us together whenever everything else failed.

Yet, in so many places our lives were still out of balance—with God, with people, and with each other. Because of what I call "dysfunctional living skills" which we both acquired in our childhood, we fought against almost impossible odds. But now for the first time, and because we had Christ, we had something that gave us both hope. God provided the motivation and courage to tackle the wall of tangled emotions that encircled our lives.

We immediately set up priorities. As a first priority, we wanted to grow in our newfound faith.

We moved to Euless, Texas. We were closer to the Mid-Cities Bible Church where the Reeves attended. With our tangled up finances, we couldn't afford to buy a house, but we did rent an apartment. The Bible Church became the focal point of our family, and we attended as often as we could.

As long as B.J. and I had been married, we had both had employees. But now we had something different. In our church, we had people who cared about us—a community. Both of us had grown up in homes where no one really knew how to express love. But in that church we felt like part of an extended family.

We developed friendships within the church. For the first time in my entire life, I met a network of caring people who received us as people and demanded nothing in return. I could call one of them anytime I needed to talk or wanted a favor. Once I became quite ill during the night, and B.J. was on the road. I called a church member.

She rushed over to the apartment, got Paige ready for school, made us both breakfast, and cooked my lunch before leaving.

I later read Acts 17:11 where it speaks about the Berean believers. I paraphrased it and applied it to our Christian family: "They were most blessed because they received the Bible eagerly, they examined it daily, and made it real in their lives."

In time we could no longer maintain the closeness with all the people because of the demands of a public career. But we'll always be grateful for those days when they taught us, simply by the way they lived, what Christian community is.

Like starving children, we couldn't get enough. We had so far to go, and we wanted to grow so fast. And we saw progress in our lives.

We weren't fully in tune, but we had moments. It was as though from time to time we hit enough of the right notes that we knew what the musical score should be.

We both realize now that God only requires us to walk in the amount of light we have. In the beginning we had no patience with ourselves. When we harmonized for a few hours, we rejoiced. When we hit sour notes by losing our tempers, we felt guilty and cursed ourselves for our weaknesses. Yet we made enough progress that we kept on.

We read books, attended seminars, and listened to as many preachers and speakers as we could. It took time before we could discern the quality of information we received. In the beginning, we drank in every word without question. But through the growing process, we began seeing discrepancies between teachers and groups. We asked God to help us understand. And as we understood, we determined to settle for nothing less than a total commitment of our lives to Christ.

As our second priority, we reestablished B.J.'s career. We needed to generate income before we could straighten out our financial morass. We quickly learned that simply because we came to the Lord didn't mean our problems disappeared.

Nothing had really been changed by our conversions. Nothing, except us. Now we could learn to cope, but the problems didn't go away.

For instance, we owed the IRS a tremendous sum. As one friend said, "That's more than many people make in their lifetime."

For weeks B.J. struggled over filing for bankruptcy. We were now Christians. How would this affect our integrity? What would the news media do with this morsel of information? We knew only that we had to make a decision and we had to do it soon.

How had we gotten into such a mess? It was easy to see our mistakes, but not quite so easy to correct them. During those drug-crazed years B.J.'s business managers, agents, and lawyers had signed him for many questionable deals; it took us five years to clear them all up. Even after our conversion, our financial records changed hands at least six times. We had no idea of what was going on. Our managers and lawyers had the power to sign contracts on B.J.'s behalf. They did whatever they saw fit to do. One especially big deal involved a contract for records.

But B.J., in one of his most violent drug-induced moods, called the president of the company and swore at him for almost an hour, saying the most unbelievable things.

The president demanded we fulfill the album contract.

We didn't know what to do. We couldn't go forward until we cleared up the current mess. We had to generate some kind of money flow.

When B.J. mentioned bankruptcy to me, I was opposed to the idea. I had always survived every crisis by fighting my way through it. B.J. had been taught to run. I accused him of running again.

"This isn't running. This is facing the problem."

"You do what you want," I said and meant it. "I'll support any decision you make."

B.J. made his decision and finally declared bankruptcy. Later, I realized it was the only way to begin the straightening-up process.

But even declaring bankruptcy wasn't simple. Our battery of lawyers charged us ninety thousand dollars (which the judge agreed to). We received at least a dozen pages listing our financial debts. Of that endless list, only two were deals we had personally and consciously entered into.

In an unprecedented decision, the judge terminated the contract with the record company. B.J. hung on to his manager and his agent so that he could work enough to pay the lawyers, then he could afford to go bankrupt!

From that time on, we began moving slowly down the path of financial integrity. Our manager still made several bad deals (which did not come to light until much later), but we were moving forward.

The concert bookings came—with a "new" B.J. singing. During his concerts B.J. had begun to introduce religious songs into the program. More than that, he would stop in the middle of the show and talk for a few minutes to the audience. Every time he spoke, it was always different. And knowing the sincerity of my husband, it was always from his heart.

At his first concert in Atlanta, he said, "You know, this is the first time I've ever seen the faces of the audience. For so many years I've come out on stages like this, and I was always stoned. I was so caught up in my drugs I never saw people. I was flying high. But one day God made a change in my life, and I'm different now."

While performing at Six Flags Over Texas, he said, "I'm a Christian who's an entertainer, but I'm not a Christian entertainer. I plan to keep singing the songs I've always sung as well as new ones both pop and gospel. When you buy a ticket, I want to give you an hour of cheer and make you feel better."

The audience responded with tremendous applause. They sensed the reality of his words.

During the engagement at Six Flags Over Texas, a representative from Word Records came to the show. He had heard about B.J.'s conversion experience and wanted to find out for himself. As a result of hearing B.J. that night, he got in touch with us, and we signed a contract to record contemporary gospel music with Word.

Word began to promote their new singing star. They arranged press conferences all over the country to introduce B.J. to the Christian community. In the publicity they emphasized, "Pop-singing drug addict, born again."

Overall, the Christian community accepted us. People across the country told us how, over the years, they had been impressed to pray for my husband. It always touched us to hear such statements. The criticisms came later. But in the early days, we felt accepted. We were making headway in our lives and beginning to bring them into tune.

B.J.'s first album for Word, *Home Where I Belong,* was a special project, born of love and sincerity. It provided his first chance to tell the Christian community of his belief and joy.

The Lord blessed B.J.'s ministry through that album. *Home* was a million-seller, which is unheard of in gospel music.

Later, it was nominated for a Grammy Award. B.J. won. And through that win, we felt God was confirming his career.

That same record attracted the attention of the MCA people. They approached B.J. with a contract for pop records, which he signed. His first pop album hit the top of the charts. It featured the old classic made famous by the Beach Boys, "Don't Worry, Baby."

Yet even with the fame from high sales, people didn't have a clear image of B.J. The black radio stations played his records—in the days when not many white acts made the rhythm-and-blues charts. They referred to him as our "blue-eyed soul brother."

He had become a leader within the business itself. The Rolling Stones told him that when they travel they play all of his records again and again. Other big names in the business lauded him for his style and ability.

Kenny Rogers once said to Paige, "Your daddy is the greatest living singer I know."

Another friend called him "B.J. Thomas—superstar."

We often laughed, even though we felt some frustration. B.J. *was* a superstar—but a secret superstar. The public still associated him with "Raindrops" but little else. Yet among his peers, he is known as the songwriter's singer.

And what a change in B.J.'s reputation. Instead of unstable and undependable, he became known as "One-take Thomas." At recording sessions, he would have an entire album wrapped up in two or three days. In contrast, it is not uncommon for recording artists to take sixteen hours for a single song.

We were moving upward. And God smiled on B.J.'s career. We saw that God had given him the talent. We also had a sense of mission. We had a reason to live and a message to spread.

In one conversation I said, "I feel as though we've fallen out of the sky, and we're now starting down the Yellow Brick Road to Oz."

"At least we know we're headed in the right direction," B.J. answered.

We didn't have all the answers. We made mistakes. But we were on the way.

8

Growing in the Faith

We thought we had entered Paradise after our conversions. But even the Garden of Eden had a snake. The euphoria evaporated when we saw that Christians could behave as badly as other people. In several instances, conflicts arose among Christians because of our newfound relationship with Jesus Christ.

In this chapter, I want to explain about the major conflicts we encountered. Most of them centered around relationships.

Paige and me. In 1976, B.J. and I started to come to grips with reality. For nearly two years prior to that, Paige had shifted for herself emotionally. B.J. was gone most of the time and stoned when he *was* around. We argued, screamed, and slugged. I had been almost a basket case myself. Paige, a rather passive child, had stored up anger that she did not understand. A tension developed between the two of us, and often B.J. had to step in and arbitrate. For me, the bottom line to the conflict became suppression and control.

Partially because of the religious environment and teaching, and partially because I didn't know how to cope better, I suppressed my negative feelings. I controlled Paige as much as possible with demands and threats. I felt constantly angry at her, not understanding why or how we had fallen into the conflict. Slowly I began to see that the conflicts between Paige and me mirrored my own sad family experiences. But for a long time I still had no idea how to cope. Not until a later trip we were to take to Israel did I see a glimmer of hope.

Yet in those days immediately after our conversion, while I dreamed of our family unity, Paige grew more distant. I had tried to enforce my will, believing I was right. I often quoted, "Train up a child in the way he should go: and when he is old, he shall not depart from it" (Proverbs 22:6). I determined to make her conform to my concept of the right way. The tension increased.

Guilt overwhelmed me. I felt like the tropical fish who give birth to their young and, if they're not separated, turn around and eat them.

Most of all I felt like a failure.

I believe Paige felt that she had her dad back, only to find herself emotionally deserted by her mother. That was the only way I could cope. I backed off emotionally and denied my feelings of anger and frustration.

Role expectations. In some ways, this proved the most traumatic conflict of all. Almost immediately after joining the Christian community, people pounded into our heads the absolute husband and wife roles.

"B.J. is responsible for you to God. Even for your sins," one Christian repeatedly said. "You must submit to him."

"In everything?"

"As a wife, yes. *In everything.*" She underscored the last two words.

I didn't understand that teaching. My own family life had been anything but a submissive mother–dominant father situation. But the Christians around me patiently explained what they called "God's plan for family relationships."

According to them it went like this: God created the husband to be the head of the household—a rigid fact without any discussion. It worked like a chain of command in the military. God first, and Jesus submitting to Him. Then the husband bowing to Jesus. As the chain went on, the wife yielded to husband, and the children obeyed both parents. They kept referring to places in the Bible such as Ephesians 5:21–33.

I tried to argue, but I had no Bible verses. After all, I had only just begun my spiritual journey. In the early days it never occurred to me that they had oversimplified or made ironclad laws out of cultural situations.

I listened. Questioned. Balked. But when I fought back, I paid the price in guilt. I tried to submit to B.J. I agonized over my lack of buckling under.

"God, forgive me for not being a godly wife," I'd pray. "Teach me to submit."

How many times a day did I pray those words? A hundred maybe. But I kept on praying and kept trying to become submissive.

Becoming submissive meant a drastic personality change in me. I was a survivor. A fighter. I had survived because I lashed back and allowed no one to get the better of me.

"Is that what the Bible means by becoming a new creature in Christ?" I often asked.

"Exactly," my friends told me.

"You must learn to submit if you are going to follow God."

"Then why did God make me a fighter?"

I don't remember all the answers people gave me. I remember only that my new friends reminded me daily of my failure to yield myself to God because I could not yield myself to my husband.

"God, change me," I pleaded.

But I didn't change.

The guilt increased.

Only much later could I find my way out of a rigid system of conduct that I now realize caused much damage to our spiritual growth.

Yet, there I was, a new Christian, trying to get my own life in tune with God, struggling with business problems that could have wiped us out, and hearing Christian friends yelling at me to submit to B.J.

I finally gave in—I couldn't fight the people who had befriended me and taught me so much. And with their help, I had come a long way.

Okay, God, I'll be the submissive wife who bakes bread and cooks all the meals. I'll stay at home and have the place clean and tidy when B.J. comes off the road.

Bev had been working part-time for us, carrying out most of the household duties. Her two oldest sons were in high school. Her own expenses mounted, and she needed a full-time job. Instead of increasing her hours, I responded to the guilt and tried to be what I thought was the godly wife.

"I'm going to let you go, Bev," I said.

"I don't want to leave you—"

"I can handle the house. After all, that's what God created me for . . ."

Bev didn't argue. She knew I had made up my mind. Instead, her eyes filled with tears.

Hurriedly I explained, "God created me, a woman, to be a homemaker and to please my husband in everything. That means staying at home and . . ."

I rambled on for a long time, knowing that if I could talk long enough I wouldn't end up crying.

"And, besides, you need a full-time job," I finally said.

And Bev left.

I tried to juggle everything. I spent a lot of time getting our business straight. B.J. couldn't help much because he spent most of his time on the road. He came home to relax, not to haggle over business ventures. Our previous managers had made such a mess of things, we could not, as yet, trust anyone to do the work. And much of the work required traveling and being away from home.

Opportunities opened up for me to expand my talents as a songwriter. A friend who was also an executive at MCA called me one day. "Hey, Gloria, we've got a new series coming up. We need a theme song. Interested in writing it?"

"Am I!"

Within a few minutes we agreed on details, and I felt excited about the opportunity. I could use my talent and still be the godly housewife my friends told me I needed to be.

Unfortunately, it didn't work out like that. I found myself caught up in stacks of business correspondence and lengthy negotiations.

Paige needed me. I tried to keep house, cook, and be free from distraction when B.J. came home.

Eventually I wrote the song for the projected series. But I submitted it too late. I missed the chance.

I sank into depression, feeling I had no way out. I had no one to help me. I read about the woman in Proverbs 31. That woman seemed able to do everything. I couldn't sleep at night and would often be awake when the first rays of dawn came. That made me moody and tired the next day. More than once I lay in the silence of the room and prayed, *God, just let me die. I can't take much more of this.*

B.J. came home from a road trip, saw the circles under my eyes, and sensed the heaviness of my heart. He didn't even ask, "What's wrong?" He knew.

B.J. is not a verbal man by nature. But he's sensitive to people and to atmosphere. He just said two words: "Call Bev."

Bev was working in a factory, hated her job, and wanted out of it. I was going to call her but she dropped in that evening to see me. As I opened the door, our eyes met, and we stood immobile for a minute.

Then I lunged forward, grabbed her, and burst into tears. It took me several minutes to realize that she was crying too.

The next day Bev came back to work for us—full-time. Bev was not a Christian. But a few weeks afterward, she and her sister Jackie had come over one evening. We talked about Jesus Christ and before leaving, both of them committed their lives to Him.

"I'm so grateful for you," I said as I hugged Bev the night she decided for Christ. "You've always been like my big sister. Now you're also my sister in Christ."

Bev's coming back to work gave me a lift that pulled me out of my depression. She needed the job. I needed the help.

"You don't need to spend your time cooking and washing clothes," B.J. said.

Both of us realized that I not only needed to get out of doing the housework, but I had other things to give my energies to.

Privacy. After the release of *Home Where I Belong* (the album and book), B.J.'s career seemed back on track. More opportunities came for concerts, tours, and television. But fame had its price. We were losing our privacy.

Strangers came to our door. "We just wanted to stop by and meet you folks."

I'd feel guilty if I didn't invite them in. Yet my overcrowded schedule told me that I already had more things planned for each day than I could accomplish.

Paige was being used by people as a way to get in to see us. They'd strike up a friendship with her and then come over to our house. The phone calls increased. Dozens of letters came from fans every day. We got so that we didn't want to hear the phone or the doorbell ring.

"We've got to get out of this place," I said to B.J.

He agreed.

We were still in the midst of tax problems and the bankruptcy proceedings, so we knew it would not be easy to find the capital. But with the help of understanding Christian friends we found a house in a Dallas suburb. Eventually we moved in, shutting ourselves away from prying eyes.

Judy. In my entire life I've really hated only one person: Judy, B.J.'s sister. Whenever she came to see us, I felt like a total outsider. We could hardly give each other a civil word. Usually as soon as she and B.J. started to talk, I walked out.

Had it not been for Jo Ellen, I wonder if I would ever have dealt with my hostility toward Judy.

Jo Ellen, then a member of the Mid-Cities Bible Church, was a positive person, always able to look at life with a smile on her face. She showed her friendship in hundreds of ways. For instance, she found our house for us. She also taught me much about God.

"Gloria, God cares about you. He also cares about every need you have."

She must have said that to me a hundred times. We'd talk, often for hours at a time. I always felt refreshed and stronger afterward. She wanted nothing from me, yet she was always there when I needed to talk. She never laid down rules or forced Scripture on me.

I like to think of her as a teacher, who took my hand and led me step by step over rocky terrain. When I'd hold back, she'd pull gently, encouraging me to move forward.

"God can transform lives," she'd remind me. "God works in people by getting His people to pray."

More than anything else, Jo Ellen enabled me to cope with Judy. But coping wasn't enough.

My commitment to Christ eased some of the tension in our relationship. I felt less hostility toward her, but it was far from over. And then, a few months after our conversion, Judy, too, met Jesus Christ.

Our first Christmas as Christians, 1977, was her first as well. We wanted it to be a Christian family time. B.J.'s mother, his brother, Jerry, and Judy spent the day with us. We declared an unspoken truce, and no angry words flowed.

A week later, Jerry said, "I need to tell you something. Judy's pregnant. She's too embarrassed to tell you herself."

Now a divorcée, it meant raising her child alone. She had moved in with her mother, who lived in a small farming community near Houston. B.J. and I talked it over.

"I think they need to stay with us for a while," I said. "At least until they can find an apartment nearby."

I knew that was the right thing to do. I felt pity for her and perhaps even the first stirrings of compassion. Jo Ellen helped me deal with my real feelings.

"See her through God's eyes," she'd remind me. "She's a child of God, too. She's a hurting, lonely person."

Another time she said, "God sometimes sends our worst enemies to us and expects us to treat them as we would treat Jesus Christ Himself."

"Lord, help me," I prayed over and over. "Help me accept Judy and love her."

In the end Judy moved in with us. When she did, somehow I knew it was right. And what a strange time to come. Although large, our apartment was inadequate for two families. Our budget, still tight, already had us under a strain.

We lived together two months. In those two months, we had no major blowups. I kept expecting the worst confrontations, but they never came. We had a few cross words, but then, with all of us living together, that was normal.

I couldn't believe the way Judy took the whole thing. She had a peace that I envied. I saw something in her that began to draw us together. Her whole life was up in the air. She was divorced and pregnant. She had to depend on us for everything. Judy had no idea of what she was going to do afterward or how she could stand on her own. Yet when we talked she said, "God will help me work it out."

During those two months, my feelings toward her mellowed. I no longer hated her, but I still resented her intrusion in our lives. Day after day I sobbed out the story to Jo Ellen.

One day Jo Ellen's words finally got through to me. "Gloria," she said, "your attitude is not hurting Judy. Not really. It's hurting *you.* You're getting all filled up with poison. Look at Judy. She's at peace."

Gradually I began to understand. For the next eight months, Jo Ellen spent time with me *every* day. I needed her. I couldn't have made it without her help. She helped me see that Christian love is an act of obedience, not an emotion. "You do the right thing because it's right, not because you feel good about it."

I had been programmed negatively all of my twenty-six years, but Jo Ellen helped reverse the process. "Keep seeing life and people as God sees them."

It took eight months, but by the end of that time I had learned to understand Judy. God had been at work in my heart, and I genuinely loved her. And Judy loved me.

In the years since, Judy has stepped in when I've needed emotional support. She's become very close to me and has been a wonderful sister-in-law.

Judy, like B.J. and me, had wasted her life until Christ came into the picture. She had previously worked less than two years. But she has since become a hardworking career woman, a breadwinner, and a responsive mother. But most of all, as far as I'm concerned, she is one of the closest friends I have in the world.

9

Image vs. Reality

The conflicts I faced weren't mine alone. Together B.J. and I had battles going on in other places. But these particular battles we fought side by side. In this chapter I want to tell you about three of them.

Business conflicts. Now that we could look beyond ourselves a bit, we saw that B.J.'s business manager was in deep trouble himself. Everyone on our payroll seemed to have more problems than we did. We'd fire one person, only to replace him with someone as bad —or even worse.

Unknown to us, B.J.'s manager signed a contract with the book division of Word. He accepted an advance check, and that money soon went into our confused cash flow. This particular manager manipulated B.J. He would do whatever he felt like doing and then announce the decision to B.J. and argue until he talked him into it.

One day he started talking to B.J. about writing his story. B.J. hesitated, feeling he wasn't ready. The manager, however, had ways of manipulating B.J. through subtle arguments, thrown out over a period of several days.

"The publisher can send a writer to help you."

"Look at what the Lord has already done for you. Christians need to know about it."

"Think of the potential sales—and the income from the book."

"You can make a real impact by witnessing to nonbelievers."

B.J. finally agreed. Only later did we realize that he had already signed the contract for us.

That's how the book *Home Where I Belong* came into being. It wasn't an easy time for us. Both of us were still so young in the faith. We didn't have the energy or the maturity to probe deeply. Even so, it took a lot out of B.J. to relive his story while Jerry Jenkins helped him write it.

I've since said, "We conceived and delivered that book with great labor pains from day one."

But despite the pain, God honored our efforts. We're proud of the testimony that *Home Where I Belong* makes. Even now, six years later, we still receive letters from people because our story touched their lives. So as we measure results, the pain of birthing eventually brought joy.

Our business manager left us shortly after the book appeared and has been out of our lives for almost five years. Even so, we suffered the results of his work for a long time afterward. He signed a contract with a casino in Las Vegas and accepted an advance. B.J. didn't know about the deal, and the manager never told him. We found out only when we were hit with a lawsuit.

It took us a long time to realize that this tendency to hire untrustworthy people came from unhealthy role models from our childhood. We had never been around people who functioned with integrity and ability. Consequently, we didn't know how to go about recognizing good people, let alone hiring them. Over the years, however, as we learned more about ourselves, we also saw why we kept repeating the same mistakes. Today, five years later, we have people surrounding us who are everything we didn't have during those dark years.

The Christian community. What would I have done without those wonderful Christian friends in the beginning? I think of them now as wooden planks spread over deep mud holes. I could walk over those boards, keeping my balance, and avoid the pitfalls. But the boards didn't *eliminate* the holes—they only covered them.

As we enlarged our Christian contacts, sometimes we encountered vicious, insensitive people. At first it confused us, then threw us into depression. How could this be happening? Weren't we all brothers and sisters in Christ? We tried to believe that and practice it. That led us into deep troubles.

For instance, B.J. would talk informally with several Christians after a concert. But before he had credibility with them, he'd have to pass their test.

"Do you believe in Jesus Christ, B.J.?"

"I certainly do."

"Are you convinced that if you were to die tonight, your soul would go to be with the Lord?"

"Yes," he'd answer.

After four or five more questions with right responses, the examiner would extend his hand, "You're a real Christian, aren't you, B.J.?"

On the other hand, sometimes when B.J. sensed the person was ready to spring the religious third degree, he'd speak up honestly. "I know I'm a Christian and so does God, whether you or anyone else believes it."

Then they'd accuse him of hostility.

On one occasion, a Christian writer contacted us for a two-part article. He met with us, talked to B.J., and wrote the first part. Because of heavy scheduling and an unexpected demand on our time, they never got back together for the second part.

So for the second installment the writer reflected on his impression of us. He questioned our commitment to Christ, implying that if we were genuine Christians we were still quite shallow.

More than the article, we received letters that troubled us and hurt me most of all. When the first ones came, criticizing B.J., I wrote lengthy replies, defending our position. But the letters piled up. I started with five. By the time I had finished answering the first three, I had over forty new ones. Then a hundred. They overwhelmed me.

I recall one three-page letter in particular which came from a church in Colorado. They reminded B.J. that Jesus had said, ". . . freely ye have received, freely give" (Matthew 10:8). They added,

"Since God did not charge for your gift but gave it freely, don't you have an obligation to do the same?"

The letter concluded with an invitation to sing at their church. "And, of course, we'll take up a love offering for you."

I'd read letters like that and cry with anger or frustration. All of them made me feel guilty.

B.J. helped me. "Don't let them lay that on you," he'd say when I'd tell him about a particularly hurtful letter.

I tried not to show him most of the letters. Usually he took them more personally when he read them, and then he would throw a temper tantrum.

"Who do these people think they are?"

I'd try to calm him down. "B.J., they just don't understand."

"They sure don't. They never criticized me when I lived on drugs."

"They didn't listen to your singing either."

"But they're unfair!"

"And shallow, too," I added.

Sometimes he'd brood for days. He tried so hard to follow Christ's teachings. "If Christians can't understand me, how can I expect other people to react?"

He was right; we didn't get critical letters from non-Christians. The poison-pen letters all came from church people.

One incident that hurt deeply involved the picture for the album, *For the Best.* The photographer wanted to catch B.J. singing, as he put himself into his music. B.J. personally liked that cover because it caught a true expression of his feelings when he sang.

His critics disagreed.

Aside from letters sent directly to us, a vitriolic attack came out of the "Feedback" section of a Christian magazine. One writer said, "I laughed out loud when I saw the new B.J. Thomas album *For the Best* on MCA Songbird. Perhaps I should have cried: It is so obvious he is being made to appear tough to sell the album. That snarl makes him look like he is in pain, maybe he has hemorrhoids or something."

Others responded in support of B.J. in later issues of the magazine. One said, "The singers look silly, huh? Great, so don't buy their albums. . . . The pained look B.J. Thomas has on his face was put there by Mr.—— and his kind, so quick to find fault and eager to undo whatever good someone else might accomplish."

"Can't they understand?" B.J. screamed over one unkind letter. "I haven't moved out of this world! I'm a Christian, but I still sing for people—not just for a few people gathered in a church somewhere!"

We were both new in the Christian faith. We had no other patterns of behavior to follow except anger. And I, especially, had learned to strike back when in pain or when attacked.

After one particularly ugly letter, B.J. said, "You're trying to please those narrow-minded people, Gloria. And they don't understand. They just can't understand."

"But it affects our testimony."

"It shows them as ignorant."

Another time a man burst into the dressing room and, giving a full grin, stuck out his hand and said, "Brother Thomas, I don't mean to be rude, but I'm a Christian!"

B.J. looked up at him and said slowly, "So you're a rude Christian!"

The toothy grin disappeared, and so did the man.

Christians would burst in on us, assuming that because we both serve Jesus Christ that automatically gave them the right to invade our privacy.

We had bright moments, too, however—

One person (I assume a woman from the handwriting) wrote inside the cover of a book she left, "For your benefit, I haven't added my name or address."

"Look!" I squealed. "Someone who wants nothing in return!"

And every day for at least three months I prayed for that wonderful Christian out there!

Christian promoters. Christian promoters signed contracts and then would not pay. We learned fairly early in the business—as most artists have to, the hard way—to get the money up front.

One time two ministers rented a music hall and advertised B.J.'s concert in both the secular and religious media. We had a signed, legal contract as we would with anyone else. They refused to pay B.J. before he went on.

"Sorry, but we just don't have the money," one of the ministers said.

B.J.'s brother, Jerry, who has always been our road manager, said, "You pay or he doesn't go on."

"But we don't have the money!"

"Then B.J. doesn't go on. We have a binding contract with you."

"But isn't this a ministry?" the other minister asked.

"No, this is a business," B.J. answered. "I didn't leave my family behind, travel halfway across the United States, pay for all my people to come with me, so that I could have church with you."

B.J. held his ground. In all but three instances, they came up with the money and he went on. In those three cases, they protested, "But we'll take up a love offering."

"My contract says nothing about a love offering," he would remind the promoter.

Then the criticism: "You don't have much of a relationship with the Lord to walk out on a concert."

"You must not have much of one either, because you want to cheat me."

These were painful, soul-searching times. But our close Christian friends rallied around us, easing the hurt and the criticism. One time the pastor's wife's face turned red when she heard of an incident. "That makes me so angry," she said, "so angry I could cry."

Another woman said, "If people treated me that way I couldn't handle it. You two don't seem to let it get you down."

In reality, the critical letters never numbered anywhere near those that thanked B.J. for ministering to them through his music. It's just that, being young and trying to follow Christ, we tended to let the letters of criticism sting us and overshadow the others.

At one point in late 1981, B.J. had been interrupted in his dressing room by two women who criticized his manner of "sexy" singing and his choice of "worldly songs." They also said, "The Lord told us to tell you."

B.J. stared at the women and said, "God didn't tell you any such thing! You don't like my music and you told me. But don't blame it on God."

Later he realized his temper had gotten the best of him. "Maybe I'll learn, Gloria, maybe I'll learn."

The next day we received a letter from a woman in Florida. With her permission I am quoting the entire letter:

November 13, 1981

Dear Mr. Thomas,

I was at the concert you and Andraé Crouch gave at the Jacksonville Coliseum about two years ago. I was one of the people who got up and left when you sang the secular songs. At the time, I felt that I was correct to do this, but it has bothered me ever since, and I have prayed about it and thought about it a *lot.* Those old songs brought back a lot of memories in my life that I had tried to forget—some good and some bad, and I had just wanted to hear the songs I bought your albums for—the ones about the Lord we both love.

I now feel that I was *very* wrong and very rude to leave. I pray you will forgive me and the others who left, too. We are all just learning in this life to be more like Jesus. I really am *so* sorry!!

Please be patient with us, and *don't give up* in your ministry! We love you. I'm praying for you.

Your sister

We wish everyone would—and could—understand like this woman. We'll probably still keep getting irate letters and sharp criticisms from people.

The criticisms hurt most of all because they come from people who serve the same Jesus Christ that we do.

10

Up in Smoke

Slowly we began to get our lives in tune with Jesus Christ and with each other. It hasn't always been easy.

Many times we fell backwards. Yet somehow we sensed that our setbacks were only temporary.

During this early period, among our ups and downs we had one experience that could have caused an absolute disaster.

It started with our smoking.

Although both of us had smoked heavily for years, we thought nothing about it until months after our conversion. Looking back now, I marvel at the way our Christian friends tolerated us.

We began to think seriously of the implications of verses such as 1 Corinthians 10:31, "Well, whatever you do, whether you eat or drink, do it all for God's glory" (TEV).

Or this one: "Don't you know that your body is the temple of the Holy Spirit, who lives in you and who was given to you by God? You do not belong to yourselves but to God; he bought you for a price. So use your bodies for God's glory" (1 Corinthians 6:19, 20 TEV).

We'd be sitting in a Christian group, and I'd light up. I've always been open about my feelings, and I decided that as long as I smoked I would do it publicly.

Publicly, yes, but also with much guilt. And the guilt grew.

Thinking back, I realize now that I excused myself by saying, "One of these days the Lord will deliver me from these little things, but in the meantime . . ." And I'd inhale again.

B.J. and I tried to quit. We tried everything. The Shick method. Self-denial. A friend would suggest a method, and we would give it a try. But we always went back to smoking again. I had begun to think we'd never lick the habit.

More than once B.J. and I talked about our mutual habit.

"It's hard to believe," he said. "I quit drugs with no trouble. I just quit. But I can't seem to kick nicotine."

"I don't understand either," I said.

B.J. had quit drugs cold turkey. And contrary to all the stories we'd heard and warnings we received, he never had drug flashbacks. Not once. The first three months we kept waiting for one to occur.

"A great miracle like that," I said, "and we can't overcome a small habit like cigarettes."

One night we visited in the home of a local evangelist. As usual, both of us smoked our cigarettes as we talked about what Jesus Christ had done for us.

Finally the evangelist said, "You know, folks, God wants to set you free from that habit."

"We've tried to quit," B.J. said.

"Several times," I added.

"You sure don't glorify God by the way you're ruining your bodies."

"We've really tried," B.J. said again.

"God can do it for you."

He kept talking, as though he had to convince us of our need to quit. We only needed help.

"I want to pray for you. I believe God can set you free."

He prayed for us for several minutes. I didn't feel anything and I didn't know how B.J. felt.

B.J. stood up, took a half-filled pack of cigarettes out of his shirt pocket, squashed the package, and dumped it in a wastebasket. I took out my cigarettes and did the same thing, but not because I felt delivered. I simply didn't want my husband to leave me behind.

As simple as that experience was, God met us. We have never smoked since.

Friends who had already been talking to me about nutrition urged me to take large doses of vitamins, especially C. I did. B.J., on the other hand, saw no value in the vitamins and wouldn't take any.

Two days later we flew to Orlando, Florida, for B.J. to perform at the "Jesus '78" conference. I had noticed he was moody, but didn't give it a lot of thought. He sometimes got that way before a big performance. But on the plane, I realized what was happening.

B.J. went through a chemical withdrawal. It hadn't happened when he gave up drugs after his conversion. But in the earlier years when he'd try to "dry out," he'd have those drug flashbacks. He'd act as if he had just taken a handful of uppers. He would become irrational, talkative. His language was abusive. If I tried to talk to him during those times, he'd hit me, often knocking me down.

When we got off the plane, two ministers met us with their warm smiles and stretched-out hands.

Immediately B.J. swore at them. "What kind of people are you? Maggots or something?" He let a string of unprintable words fly.

One shocked minister said, "Look here, brother, what we're doing here is for the Lord."

"Yeah? Is that why you charge people ten dollars to park their cars?"

Somehow we managed to get him out of the airport and into the waiting car. He screamed and yelled at them the whole time. He brought up every rotten thing any Christian had ever said or done.

We finally got him backstage. I knew beyond question what had happened. "Please, listen, this isn't B.J. talking. He's having a drug flashback."

I don't know if they believed me at first or not. But I knew B.J. had changed. I couldn't let them think he was still an addict.

One of the ministers walked over to B.J., laid his hand on him, and started praying.

"What do you think you're doing?" B.J. yelled out, but he didn't remove the man's hand. The minister kept praying. Soon others gathered around us and prayed. They asked the people attending the festival to pray. Thirty thousand hearts united in prayer.

Later, when B.J. went on stage, the drug flashback had changed him like a chameleon. All the symptoms had not passed, yet they were chaneled into a positive spiritual high. B.J. did not sleep for three days, but his attitude changed completely. He was the new B.J. Thomas again. He sang with a vitality I had never heard before. He was as high on the spiritual level as he ever had been on drugs. For the rest of the road trip, B.J. stayed on that high plane. He did the best singing of his career.

One by one, we were putting into practice the things God had taught us through experience and through people like Jo Ellen. The mountains were now becoming only small hills. We were getting our lives in tune, because we were singing the Lord's song.

Our finances improved. After four months and five turndowns, a mortgage company accepted our application. We closed the deal on our new house in May of 1978. It had been five years since we'd left our lovely home in Connecticut. This time it was different. We didn't move into just a new house. This was home—*our home.*

For two months, during the summer of 1978, we spent all of our spare time getting ready to move. We had family time together and enjoyed just the routine of packing, discarding, discussing, and re-packing.

Then another opportunity came.

In August B.J., Paige, and I were going overseas—our first time. B.J. had signed a contract to sing at a crusade in Taiwan. We decided that after the crusade we would fly to Israel and Greece for a vacation. We looked forward to it, planned for it, and talked about it almost daily.

That trip probably did more to change our lives than anything else. Of course, we had no way of knowing that before we went.

We knew only that we had accepted an invitation to go to Nationalist China with a sweet and bubbling lady, Nora Lam Sung.

11

Nora Lam Sung's Crusade

The Nora Lam Sung crusade included a large number of singers, ministers, and trained counselors. She held children's crusades in the afternoon and evangelistic services in the evening aimed at the whole family.

We all met at the San Francisco airport. When we arrived at our departure area, we saw Nora fluttering from person to person, excited and having her picture snapped by guests and onlookers. B.J., Paige, and I became as excited as the rest of them.

Then the flight began. By the time we had reached Taiwan, twenty-four hours of flying time later, we were exhausted. The long ordeal through customs tried the patience of the ministers as much as the rest of us.

We came out of the airport, and the fresh air made us feel as though we had walked into an open-air steam room. While the temperature was only about eighty-five degrees, the heavy humidity drained us of our remaining energy.

Little girls ran up to us, handing each of us flowers. We saw a red carpet spread before us, leading to a hastily erected podium, miked for sound. Nora, and those who spoke their greetings after her, all said how glad they were to finally arrive in free China.

Immediately cars whisked us to the Grand Hotel, appropriately named and one of the finest I've ever been in. We marveled at the unusual landscaping, particularly the shrubs, shaped like animals, baskets, or symbols we didn't recognize. The hall and stairways were mammoth, giving the impression of walking into a palace. At least fifteen beautiful bonsais decorated the lobby.

Even the ballroom and meeting rooms for the press conferences were elaborate, with hand-carved woodwork.

Under the entire ground floor, the hotel houses a shopping area and several restaurants. From the higher floors, we could see the high, bamboo fences, encircling and guaranteeing privacy to the small homes nearby. The gardens, rather than sprawled out in rows, were a series of tiers, all on lattices, reaching skyward. The warm temperature and constant humidity produced an abundance of flowers and greenery.

We held the crusade in Taipai, the largest city in Taiwan. We encountered all kinds of problems. We had expected some difficulty with the language barrier and were not mistaken. The worst of all for us happened the first night.

B.J. got up to sing "Raindrops." We had come with a live-to-mike tape which B.J. sang to. It had seemed the most sensible way to do it and eliminated having to carry extra people and equipment. B.J. started the second stanza and suddenly the tape broke.

Not missing a beat, B.J. continued a cappella. Later he said to me, "The peace of the Lord came over me, and I didn't worry at all."

After the service, one of the American pastors came up to B.J. and said, "You know, I've been wondering about you all along. Not sure if you were really a Christian or not. But when you kept on singing after that tape broke, I knew. That convinced me like nothing else that you were a committed Christian."

B.J. smiled politely and thanked the man. At the same time he felt frustrated that he kept having to prove his conversion to people. "Why can't they just accept my word for it? I don't make them prove anything."

Yet despite our own personal bad start with the broken tape, the crusade went smoothly. With all the hassles and confusion, we witnessed over a hundred thousand Taiwanese make professions of faith in that four-day period. Seeing the people milling toward the front touched me. "It's the most beautiful sight in Taiwan," I whispered to the woman who sat next to me.

When we agreed to go to Taiwan, our first of many crusades outside the United States, we expected that no one would even know B.J. We were wrong. They knew him and his music. Wherever we went people recognized him. We frequently heard Chinese, young and old, sing "Lainlops keep fallin' on my head."

While there, we developed relationships with several people. Most especially, we got to know Patty Roberts, who was then married to Richard, Oral Robert's singing son. A beautiful singer in her own right, she radiated a relationship to Christ that drew me to her. We spent some of our free time together.

One afternoon, Paige and I were having lunch in the Grand Hotel. Nora Lam came in and sat down at our table. In her delightful way she looked at the waiter and said, "I'll have the salad," and with hardly a pause in between she turned to me. "And I have a baby for you."

"A baby? For me?" I hardly knew what to say.

"God told me so," she said, and sipped a glass of water. I could tell by her eyes, she was playing no game with us. For Nora the matter was quite simple. God had told her we were to adopt an orphan over whom she had custody. In simple obedience, she told us.

"Terrific," I said. "Now talk to B.J."

That was the end of our conversation about a baby. Later that day she gave me more details, but was still vague. I knew only that she had a Korean baby girl who needed a family. Nora had found the twelve-day-old orphan on her previous trip.

I told B.J. about the conversation.

"Nora Lam has a baby for us," I said.

"What? You crazy?"

"Well, you've been saying you want another child. I didn't think it would matter where it came from."

He stared at me and said nothing more.

By now I had learned how B.J.'s mind worked. "Think about it," I said and dropped the subject. I knew he really would think about it.

"You haven't committed us to anything?"

"Of course not," I said.

In the next two days he mentioned the subject again, but I played it down. "It's your decision."

The Taiwan crusade over, we all prepared to leave the next day. Nora and others went to Hong Kong and then on to Singapore before returning to the States. Patty Roberts left for Calcutta, India. We began our vacation in Israel and Greece.

Aside from the anticipation of the vacation, B.J. was glad to leave Taiwan. The humidity had affected his health. He was dehydrated, had no appetite, and was irritable. Even during those four days in Taiwan, we had some flare-ups between us. But they were minor compared with the yelling bouts we still had from time to time.

On our way to Israel we had to change planes in Manila. At that stopover a profound change began taking place in my life. I had no idea how deeply it would change me and my attitude.

I said to someone later, "Emotionally we had come to the end of our rope. Our trip became a crash course in rope weaving in midair."

During our layover we deplaned and decided to walk around the airport. A full-scale argument broke out between us. Other people in the area wouldn't have recognized it as a fight. We had learned to disguise our hostility. We spoke in normal tones. Even our faces hid much of the anger.

But we knew. We knew each other so well.

I can't remember what triggered it off. In those days it didn't take much. Both of us were programmed for conflict, so our differences surfaced easily.

When stressful situations arose, B.J. lashed out at me as though I should have solved the problem. Or anticipated it and settled everything in advance.

I had heard angry words for so long that they had little effect on me. But I had just as many well-chosen words for him.

Yet, even with my retort, I accepted the irrational premise of being at fault. I felt responsible for his misery. I had failed B.J. again and hadn't lived up to his expectations. It didn't matter that no human being could have lived up to such unrealistic thinking.

I fought back—but the anger only covered a deep-seated guilt. In retrospect, I realize both of us lived in a fantasy world of confusion. As long as we followed our pattern, we could never conquer our problems.

We returned to our plane, the anger still between us. But something happened inside me.

We can't go on living this way, I said to myself. *We've got to find a better way.*

I had no idea how or when the change would occur, but in those minutes before takeoff from Manila, I felt a peace within. Somehow our lives would change. *I knew it.* We would learn to cope without anger at every new development.

Then a new thought hit me. That one thought opened a door for both of us that eventually led to harmony in our lives. It took a long time before I understood how to use the insight that came to me in that moment. But I suddenly understood the basic cause of our trouble—

We were only reacting to a pattern. We always took the same positions. B.J. blamed me. He expected me to handle and solve the problems. I reacted by feeling guilty, and when that happened, I fought back. The topic didn't matter. Whether we talked about plane schedules or dinner menus, the fights all sounded the same.

And they were the same!

We were living the way we had been taught to cope since childhood. Why hadn't I seen that before? It was so obvious, yet neither of us had recognized that the dysfunctional living patterns taught in our homes had become the patterns we followed as adults.

At that airport I had not yet seen the implications of that insight. But I knew that we couldn't change our behavior until we changed our patterns of reacting to situations.

I prayed, *God, with Your help, we can make this change!*

12

The Holy Land

Eventually we arrived in Israel, tired from the trip. B.J. had not fully recovered from the effects of Taiwan. Yet before we could think about resting we had to go through strict customs.

Clearing customs in Israel is an experience different from anywhere else in the world. Military people filled the open building, and we saw guns everywhere. We understood the need for precaution by a country at war with its neighbors, but that still did not speed up the process.

I thought we would never finish as they unpacked and repacked every single item in our thirteen suitcases. We also underwent a body search.

In that stuffy airport, pressed against crowds of people, we stood in line for over an hour. Poor B.J. Sweat dripped from his face as we left. I could tell by the way he walked that B.J. was in a terrible mood. He said nothing. I carefully guarded my own tongue. Fortunately we had no blowup between us.

A driver met us, picked up our luggage, and took us to our hotel. We checked in and wanted only one thing: a few hours of sleep in a real bed.

We slept until late afternoon. When we got up, we felt a little more refreshed and ready to enjoy Israel.

Yet, before we even left our hotel room we had words again. Who started them? It didn't matter. It never did. Again the old patterns of blaming, arguing, and threatening took over.

We ended up yelling at each other for ten or fifteen minutes but nothing more. I suddenly felt embarrassed in front of our daughter. After all our years together as husband and wife, we still couldn't handle this situation any better. I had grasped an understanding in Manila, but did not yet have the ability to put that newfound knowledge into practice. Yet I did feel less defensive this time. And less guilty.

Paige, as usual, didn't seem upset. She had grown up with this kind of behavior around her and had developed an adultlike tolerance for her childlike parents.

After the venom had died out, B.J. stopped and said, "Let's not ruin our vacation this way."

"We're acting just like we do at home," I said, and realized I was on the verge of tears. "We wanted this trip to be special."

For a moment B.J. said nothing. Then he took my hand. "Let's stop fighting. Instead let's just dive into the Bible and read together."

I agreed.

We unpacked our Bibles and spent time reading aloud together. Without saying it, both of us felt remorseful. By the time we finished, we were sobbing.

B.J. held me, "I don't want to fight anymore. I love you too much."

"I know," I said. Between sobs I asked his forgiveness.

"We'll make it up," we promised each other. And we meant it.

"We'll make it up to you, too," we promised Paige.

The three of us stood together, wrapped in each other's arms. A sense of peace swept over me. I pulled them both tighter and kissed their cheeks. In that moment, I sensed how good life could be for all three of us. I also sensed that it would happen. Together we'd fight our way out of the utter blackness and stand in the bright sunlight of God's love.

I've heard people talk about light bulbs turning on inside their heads. That's what happened to me in that hotel room.

As I felt B.J.'s arm tightening around me, nonverbally saying once again how much he loved me, a thought raced through my head: *I am a victim.* I had never thought of that before.

An instant later, a second thought hit me: *B.J. is every bit as much a victim as I am.*

Victim? I had never thought of that word before—especially in our own lives. Yet, immediately I understood. We were victims of dysfunctional living skills we had learned from childhood. It was as though someone had written a movie script, and we followed every line. We had been shaped by our backgrounds, and neither of us knew how to behave differently.

And for the first time I could understand myself, B.J., and our life together. We loved each other—neither of us has ever doubted that. But at times we also hated each other.

Before we went out, I sat in the silence of the room, calm and aware that a change was taking place in me. I took a pen from my purse and sheets of hotel stationery and tried to write on paper the way I felt. That moment of self-discovery, called "The Incredible Shrinking Feeling," later appeared in *Contemporary Christian Music* magazine.

Sometimes, I wonder what life would be like if I did not have to feel like a germ every so often. That inescapable feeling of shrinking to the mentality of a one-cell parasite. This does not mean that I would trade my life. The good points outweigh the bad and there is hope for a continual improvement. I realize that I am truly blessed. Is this feeling of shrinking so small really necessary?

I try to dwell on the positive side of life as in "count your blessings." This positive attitude at times can and does produce guilt feelings when I am displeased with a certain aspect of my life. To get over the "aren't you ever satisfied?" question usually is not difficult unless of course my self-esteem is the size of a germ.

If we do live our lives as a link or stairstep to a higher understanding of life, can we afford not to persistently improve the quality of our life? We can improve our circumstances to the extent that we have control over them. So many of our circumstances we do not have control over. For example, the weather, being fired, illness or accident. It is reasonable to assume that the answer lies in our responses to our circumstances.

After thinking through my situation, there is relief in knowing I have my focus in the right direction. There is also some relief in knowing I do not have to deal with anything smaller than a germ! As I ponder my self-image back to full size, I try to make the best of my experience. To learn lessons so that I will be able to set realistic goals. Maybe someday my mountain will become a memory. Of course realizing that the latter is larger than life!

Before long, I find myself responding to the events in my life with such wisdom, that when that certain something in life occurs that challenges my self-esteem, I'll handle the occasion with the poise of a python. Then on to bigger things, not to get smaller than a dog, a cat, or a pig.

In short: I have a dream. That dream is a goal of mine. It is not as far-reaching as the stars or moon or anything like that, but it is not one inch smaller than full size!

Before our guide arrived that morning, we read portions of the Bible about the places we expected to see. I found myself glowing with anticipation. I would soon see for myself the sacred places where the saints of old had walked.

B.J. had already said at least twice, "I don't think we're going to enjoy this trip very much."

Part of me agreed. After all, we'd already had one fight. Alone for five days with no business pressures and no outside interruptions by doorbells or phones, we could easily spend our hours yelling at each other. But another part of me said, *No, we're here. We're going to see everything and enjoy it all.*

In the past, we had blamed drugs for many of our problems. Or people who had cheated us or simply acted stupidly. We had all kinds of scapegoats. But this time we had no one else around. No pressures. No phone calls. Then why weren't we happy?

Why didn't the problems leave when the drugs left? Because we were still reacting to our confused world and following a pattern taught (unconsciously) in our homes; we had not yet realized we could change those patterns.

In those days in Israel, I saw a bigger world than the one we lived in. I saw families and people reacting to others differently than B.J. and I had ever done.

During those days I saw what I call a Middle-Eastern perspective about life. I know now that such a perspective isn't limited to one geographic sphere, but it took time before I realized that fact.

On the surface, the Israelis were an arrogant, tough people. They lived in a military state. We saw soldiers everywhere carrying machine guns and pistols. I saw another level as well.

Watching the simple acts of daily living, I gained a new insight into life and into the Bible. Ultimately, it furnished principles on which to operate our lives.

We saw this in so many different ways. B.J. and I had both come from families where angry and loud voices dominated family scenes, yet among the Israeli families we saw smiles and laughter. Instead of demand, we saw people giving of themselves. We heard simple requests made by children and, just as simply, refused by adults. All done calmly, obviously lovingly, with no signs of resentment or anger.

More than anything else, I saw a profound respect for children. Israelis treated them in a way that I thought ought to spoil them, letting them have a high level of freedom. There seemed little actual discipline. I heard no threats, yet a mother called and child came promptly. I watched families talking together, hugging, laughing, and showing affection for one another.

One day in Jerusalem we visited the traditional burial site of Jesus. As we started to enter, a man, obviously an Eastern Orthodox priest, was leaving. He saw Paige and stopped. He stooped over, grabbed her, and with his hands laid tenderly on her head, he closed his eyes and prayed. We couldn't understand a word, but we didn't need to. Tears rolled down his cheeks. Then he put Paige down, nodded to us, and moved on.

Later that same day, as we walked through the market inside the walls of Old Jerusalem, a merchant chatted with us. He looked at Paige and said, in broken English, "I will give you three hundred camels for that little one."

B.J. and I smiled at each other. Paige looked up at us both and with conviction in her eyes said, "Don't take it ya'll, okay?"

We laughed, and I hugged her. "Never, never," I whispered, suddenly filled with a fresh appreciation of this daughter I loved so much.

We stayed in a Tel Aviv hotel and returned there each evening. After dark we walked to the meeting square. Hundreds of people, all ages, sat on chairs or stairs. Their work for the day done, they had time to be neighbors and friends.

We smiled at people, and they waved back. Occasionally someone would realize we were Americans and talk to us. I don't recall any particular conversations. The content wasn't important; the open relationships we felt and saw going on impressed us.

Several times I tried to explain my feelings to B.J. I don't know if he understood or not. I stumbled and stuttered trying to verbalize what was going on around us. I knew only that I had taken a step forward in human relationships. It was one more move toward finding harmony in our lives.

Often, as we walked along, seeing the harmony and ease of people relaxing, our conversation turned to the subject of the Oriental baby. B.J. nearly always brought up the subject, and I knew he was giving it a great deal of thought.

"We can do it, Daddy," Paige said, ever optimistic.

Sometimes misunderstanding our reluctance she added, "It will be so easy. A new baby won't be any trouble. Mama will have me to help. I love babies, honest."

Another time she said, "I can bathe the baby, dress it, and I promise, I won't ever get mad if she comes into my room and breaks anything."

B.J. wisely gave us no answer. I knew him well enough to know that he wouldn't until he was sure in his own mind how he felt. More than once, however, he said, "Gloria, can we give a child like that the stability she needs?"

"I don't know," I answered honestly. "All we can do is try."

"We still fight a lot . . ."

"But we're learning. And with the Lord's help—" I broke off, not wanting to say too much. If I pushed, it would automatically bring out resistance in him. Then we would be back to our old patterns again.

One evening I finally said, "B.J., you've been wanting another child. We can have as many children as God sees fit to give us. It doesn't bother me if one of them comes from Korea."

When I said those words something happened to his eyes. A flicker only, but I knew my husband so well. He was envisioning life with a second daughter. *Our* child. Not a Korean orphan. Our own child who happened to be Korean by birth, but ours by love. She was offered to us as a gift of love—a gift from Korea instead of through my body.

B.J. said nothing. He didn't need to, I read his eyes. From that moment on, I knew I had a second daughter.

13

Greece

After five days in Israel, we flew to Greece. So much had happened to me internally during those five days in Israel that it took me months to sort it all out and put it into perspective. I had begun a new stage of my spiritual maturity. This growth became even more pronounced in Greece.

I've since said many times, "Israel's greatest resource is its citizens. They have people power—both men and women."

I immediately saw a difference in Greece. A skycap met us at the luggage pickup and started collecting our baggage. I saw that he was smashing a smaller suitcase by placing heavier luggage on top of it.

"No! Not that way," I said.

He looked at me, as though not seeing me, and added two more pieces.

"Put the heavier ones on the bottom," I said slowly, using gestures as well. I knew he spoke English, because he had talked to B.J.

In frustration I finally said, "B.J., see if you can make him understand."

My husband turned and faced the man. "Put the heavier suitcases on the bottom." He used almost my exact words. The skycap nodded, smiled, and rearranged the luggage.

I shook my head. Because I was a woman he did not listen to a thing I said. Such a difference from the sense of equality I had observed in Israel.

We checked into an Athens hotel and before either of us knew what had happened, another argument broke out.

For a moment I was crushed. "What's happened to us?" I cried. "We had such a wonderful experience in Israel. We were so in touch with each other—and now, back to the same screaming mess again!"

"I don't know," B.J. said simply, as remorseful as I.

We had both failed. Again.

I pulled away from B.J. and flung myself on the bed with my eyes closed. I silently prayed, *What's the use, God? We start making progress and then go back to the same old rut.*

God didn't give me an answer then. But I did calm down. I got up with a stronger determination than ever before. We *had* failed— I couldn't change that. But I had glimpsed the harmony our lives could produce. I knew neither of us would truly be happy until we had more of that harmony operating daily in us.

We will find it. And we'll not lose it next time, I vowed.

During the six days in Greece, we saw the historical places. We shopped for gifts and mementos. I'm not much of a tourist. I could have passed all of that by and just stayed with B.J. Outside of tours and buying expeditions, we spent time together: thinking, talking, sorting, struggling, praying, and reading the Bible together.

One day we went to the ruins of old Corinth. In preparation for the day, we read First and Second Corinthians. Almost as if we were in Israel again, we felt as if we were actually walking in the places the Apostle Paul might have touched with his sandals. We felt close to God and to each other.

Another day we went to the seashore. Statues in various stages of ruin and some undergoing restoration gave us a glimpse of the grandeur of ancient Greece. We ate peaches the size of small melons filled with sweet juice. But more than the gorgeous scenery, we were touching the deep and secret places in each other's lives.

Paige squealed and played for hours in the sand, making castles and playing fantasy games. We sat down far enough away so that we could talk privately, but close enough that we could watch her and respond to her yelled comments.

We had one of the most memorable moments in our entire marriage as the wind blew through our hair and our fingers touched the warm sand.

"I love you," B.J. said as he stroked my hair, "and I think you're the most beautiful woman I know. I've always felt that way."

"You have?"

"I love everything about you—"

"You mean, everything?"

"Everything, Gloria. Especially everything that is uniquely you."

Those few words told me something that I had not discovered in our ten years of marriage. I've always loved my husband. I loved him the moment I first met him. And despite the drug-crazed years and our separations, that love never died. I've never respected a man as much as B.J.

When he was at his worst, I knew it was the drugs and not the real B.J. The real B.J. is tender and sensitive. He has a talent that overwhelms me. Even after all these years, the way he sings a song still affects me emotionally.

I explain all of that because I felt B.J. had married beneath himself when he chose me. I had always tried to look my best for him, especially in public. Yet no matter how hard I tried, I felt I never measured up to his standards.

Not that B.J. ever said anything. But I felt inadequate. And no matter how hard I tried, I never thought I could live up to his expectations. In retrospect, I think I was trying to live up to what I assumed were his expectations of me.

On the other hand, B.J. had made false assumptions, too. He found it difficult to say, "I don't like that color on you" or "That dress makes you look fat."

He felt I was too sensitive so he'd say, "Looks okay, I guess" or "Fine."

He hesitated because he feared he'd hurt my feelings. I picked up on the lack of honesty and misinterpreted it.

But that day as we talked to each other I heard his words of love to me as though spoken for the first time. "You always look beautiful," he said.

In those quiet moments we were in tune with each other and

moved a step closer toward a fuller life together.

We stopped talking then and just held each other tight. After a few minutes he released me, and then, cupping my hands in his, we both prayed and thanked God for giving us a healthier outlook on life and toward each other.

Yet two days later, as we went through the long ordeal at New York customs, we had another rift. No loud words between us. We didn't need them. But his eyes blazed, and I cowered, feeling not only afraid but miserable for somehow failing.

Again, I can't remember how it started or even what it was about. We seldom recalled those things later.

We didn't speak much on the last leg of our trip from New York to Dallas. We had been gone two full weeks. We had met people, been enthralled with the crusade in Taiwan, impressed by the Israelis, strengthened by our days in Athens. Yet, at the same time, we had literally fought our way around the world.

"Amazing, isn't it?" I said. "Some things can be so bad and yet so good at the same time."

B.J. held my hand in a kind of unspoken truce.

I felt pangs of guilt for all the blowups in Manila, Tel Aviv, Athens, and New York. The same feelings of guilt and remorse that hit me after every battle. But at the same time, we had come back home with something we didn't have when we left. Besides the souvenirs and memories, we had changed in the right direction. We were not what we had been before.

We had moved to a new level of understanding. I had no idea where it would take us, but I knew it was right.

As I lay in bed that first night home, I thanked the Lord for the trip. As bad as the worst times had been, they had not ruined those special moments we had shared together. I reached over and laid my hand on B.J.'s shoulder. He was sleeping soundly. It didn't matter. I felt emotionally close to him, and I needed to touch him as an expression of that closeness.

"Thanks, God," I whispered.

14

Little Nora

After our globe-encircling trip, it took us three weeks at home to readjust to our world. It had never taken so long after any of the other trips. We could immediately tell some things were on their way to being different when we realized we couldn't spend so much time in front of the TV anymore. Programs we used to look forward to seeing no longer held our interest.

Less than a week after we got home, we received a letter from Nora Lam. I tore the envelope open and saw a picture of a Korean baby girl. I stared at the picture, imprinting the image of that baby in my mind. She had fine, black hair, thin and short, so that it looked as if it stood straight up. I fell in love with the baby just staring at her picture.

"Her name is Soo-me Park. But when I adopted her and brought her out of Korea, we renamed her Nora," the letter read.

Our baby had a face and a name.

B.J. had been out playing golf when the mail arrived. I had errands to run, so I placed Little Nora's picture on the kitchen table, along with the letter, and left.

When I returned, B.J.'s car was already there. I hurried inside. He was sitting at the table crying.

"What's wrong?" I asked, rushing to him and wrapping my arms around him.

"I picked up this picture," he said. "I knew then that God means for us to have her. And I couldn't help it, I started to cry."

"You mean we're going to get her?" I asked.

"I guess that's what it means," he said.

He stood up and wrapped his long arms around me. He didn't say anything for a moment. But the pressure of his arms around me told me more than any words could.

Then I started to cry too. "Our daughter!"

We laughed. We cried together. We found ourselves spontaneously thanking God. We kept passing the picture back and forth, staring at the infant's face, wishing we had her already.

When we had calmed down and begun thinking on a practical level, we called Nora Lam.

"When can we have her?" B.J. asked.

After several minutes of discussion, we realized that the soonest we could make a break in our schedule was in two weeks.

"Two weeks. Very good," Nora said, and we could visualize the smile on her face. "She will be ready for you."

We agreed that Paige and I would accompany B.J. to Nashville for a recording session, as we had planned. Then Paige and I would leave two days early and fly to San Jose where Little Nora lived.

Although we had a hectic schedule lined up, in those idle moments our minds constantly turned to Little Nora.

We asked each other dozens of questions. We questioned our own ability to care for her. We knew we would love her, but was that enough? Had we gotten our own lives straightened out so that she would grow up in the right atmosphere?

And what about Paige? How would she cope once the initial thrill of a new baby wore off? What about jealousy? Would she feel neglected?

No matter what our questions, we usually ended up with two answers—*One:* "We'll have to wait and see." *Two:* "We'll have to trust the Lord to help us work it out."

We had already arranged for Paige to have a private tutor. Terry Stewart traveled with us, making sure that Paige kept up with her work. While B.J. and I handled business affairs, Paige studied or went on private field trips to visit historic and cultural centers. We felt it necessary for her to know what it was like for the three of us to function as a family together. We wanted to do everything we could to make ourselves a harmonious family unit before Little Nora came.

I wanted to rush out and buy clothes for Nora, but I didn't know her size. And somehow, I couldn't pick out toys and clothes for a child I had not yet met.

But before we met Little Nora, B.J. had that recording session scheduled in Nashville. Those sessions are always a special time for me because I see my husband's most creative side. No matter how difficult things are at home, when B.J. gets inside the studio he's in control and a total professional. He works with other accomplished persons in a united, creative effort. That's when B.J. gets the opportunity to do what he does best: interpret a song. His interpretation never fails to inspire the others, and once B.J. sings it, he leaves his own unique mark on that song.

Ordinarily I would have been caught up in every minute of the recording session. But I don't remember much about those days. My memory is blurry up until I boarded that plane for San Jose.

Paige made no attempt to control her excitement. At last she would have a baby sister and would no longer be an only child. She had wanted Little Nora from the first moment.

Although we had talked with her often, I felt I had to talk again about the addition of a little sister.

"It won't be just the three of us anymore."

"Of course, I know that," she said. "And I can save us money, because I can be the baby-sitter when you want to go out."

Because we had a Korean family in our church, Paige had an image to relate to. She liked the Korean family. Also, she had a friend, Susan Chung, with whom she had maintained a relationship since the second grade. So she did not expect any trouble adjusting to the new baby.

I could hardly contain the excitement on the day we flew to San Jose. On the plane I felt nauseous. I dismissed it as part of the excitement. After all, picking up my new daughter was a powerful experience.

After what seemed like endless flying and slow-passing minutes, we arrived in San Jose. We had no trouble recognizing that a welcoming committee was there for our benefit. Oriental faces everywhere smiled and waved. Nora Lam Sung and her whole family had come, as well as Little Nora's nurse and at least ten people we had met on the Taiwan Crusade in August.

My eyes quickly spotted Nora holding a round bundle. She had dressed the baby in turquoise Chinese pajamas. Buried inside, I could see only her fine hair peeking over the top. I rushed to them. As I kissed big Nora hello, I reached for my baby. I had to have her in my arms.

I clasped her to my breast, and my tears began to flow. All the waiting, the pent-up emotion, and now the reality of really having her there in my arms, overwhelmed me. Paul Lam, Nora's grown son, snapped pictures of this special occasion. I was hardly aware of him, because I concentrated on this beautiful child.

I sensed that as our bodies touched, our spirits met as well. I felt a oneness with that child as though she had come from my own body and had literally been "flesh of my flesh."

Although our plane arrived at ten-thirty it was almost two in the morning before we got to the hotel and everyone left our room. All the excitement had taken its toll on me. A weakness crept over my body, and I felt as though I could go into a deep sleep.

I lay on the bed, trying to sleep, yet keeping my ears cocked for every sound Little Nora made as she lay in a crib the hotel had sent up.

I must have dozed off, although I'm not sure. Nora and Paige were in an adjoining room. I suddenly wondered if I had dressed Nora too warmly. I tiptoed into the room.

Paige stood next to the crib and was leaning over, playing quietly with Nora. Smiles covered both of their faces.

I forgot my tiredness, and the three of us played for almost two hours. We were getting to know our new child. We had eight months of her life to catch up on.

We put Nora on the carpeted floor. She crawled under the beds, fully aware that we watched every move. She even tried to pull herself up on the furniture.

"She likes us! She likes us!" Paige squealed.

"Oh, I know!"

I had worried about the adjustment Little Nora would have to make to us. My fears vanished then. She was at home from the first hour.

When we finally got to sleep that night I was really exhausted. We had to get up at six in the morning, and I wondered how I could do it. But when the hotel desk called, I jumped out of bed, instantly alert, and rushed in to check on Little Nora. She was sleeping peacefully.

Later, when Nora picked us up to drive us to the airport, I felt even more worn out than the day before. Little Nora must have weighed twenty-five pounds, and I kept picking her up and putting her down. My back started hurting, my head pounded. A wave of nausea hit me.

Lord, please—please don't let me be sick, I prayed.

Although I didn't feel any worse, I didn't feel much better. When Nora Lam arrived and hurried us to the airport, I kept my chatter bright. I didn't want her to know how sick I felt.

On the plane, we had no trouble with Nora. A friendly baby, she smiled at other passengers. Joy rushed to my face when people asked about her.

"We're taking her home to Texas. For the first time. We only got her last night," Paige told anyone who would listen.

People sitting nearby heard us and smiled or congratulated us. I heard Paige tell a woman sitting across the aisle from her, "This baby didn't come the natural way. We got her with clothes on."

I laughed and laughed, unable to stop. I was so filled with happiness over our new baby, yet I felt physically worn out.

Nora *had* come to us with clothes. But not enough to get us through the weekend. I had to buy diapers and everything she needed before I could even think about resting and catching up on my sleep.

B.J.'s schedule called for him to arrive the next morning. Paige held Nora all the way to the airport to pick him up. It was a quiet, playful ride.

When the passengers deplaned, I saw B.J. near the head of the line. He paused for a moment, searching for us in the crowd. Then he spotted the three of us. Despite his attempt at control, his eyes filled with tears. I was holding Nora so that B.J. could get a clear view of her. She wore the Chinese pajamas from the day before.

We had arranged a two-week break in B.J.'s schedule just so that we could get to know our child and adjust to her.

We set aside a special time during the second week to have a thanksgiving service to God for Nora.

First, we both sat down with Paige.

"Honey, Nora is a special child," B.J. said. "So special that God sent her to us as a Korean."

Paige was almost nine and understood.

"We're going to have to learn many lessons together. And this will be a special relationship for us."

For at least ten minutes, B.J. talked quietly to our nine-year-old daughter, explaining about differences, adjustments, and prejudice from outsiders.

Then all three of us prayed, one by one, thanking God for this gift from Korea.

From the beginning, Nora enriched our lives. She came to us singing—and in perfect pitch. She would fall asleep singing softly. Most of the time, she had the sweetest, most placid disposition I've ever seen. But once in a while—on rare occasions—her temper would flare and she would kick and scream. Her temper reminded me of B.J.'s. And we knew that we could learn more ourselves as we helped teach Nora about controlling her temper.

As our life began taking on a routine during those two weeks, I still didn't feel well. I blamed nerves, excitement, and adjusting to the new baby. Remembering it was time for my yearly physical, I made a mental note to mention it to Dr. Keller.

On the day of the examination, he pronounced me in good physical shape.

"But, you know, I've been feeling a little, uh, sick lately," I said. "Nothing serious. Mostly sick to my stomach, headaches—"

"Really?" he said, "I was going to ask if you had any symptoms to justify your enlarged uterus."

He grinned, making his whole face light up. For two years I had been trying to get pregnant. He had put B.J. and me through every possible test. He had given us vitamins and medications to build us up.

"You mean—you mean—"

"Don't get excited now," he said. His words expressed great caution, but his face gave me a different message. "You know, we still have to run tests. There are at least fifty reasons for an enlarged uterus—"

"I can hardly believe it!"

"But I'm only—well, 90 percent sure."

In our mutual excitement, Dr. Keller hugged me and sounded as happy as I was. Then he suddenly said, "Now, of course, this may be a false alarm. We won't know until the tests come back."

"How long do I have to wait?"

"Two days. I'll call you."

Driving home, I was already thinking about the baby's name. Back in 1972 when Hank Aaron hit home run number 617, beating Babe Ruth's record, we decided on a name for our next child.

"If the next child is a boy, we call him Aaron," B.J. said.

"And if it's a girl?"

"Then—then, we'll call her Erin," B.J. said.

We never discussed the matter again.

I walked into the house, greeted B.J., and said, "By the way, do you still think Erin or Aaron is a good name for a baby?"

"Yeah," he said. "What brings that up?"

"Oh, I just need to know."

He looked at me and our eyes met. "You mean—"

"Well, I'm at least 90 percent pregnant."

Without realizing what he was doing, B.J. swooped me up, kissing my face and neck again and again. He waltzed me around the room, humming Brahms' "Lullaby." I squealed and laughed, too.

Paige, in another room, overheard the racket we were making. She rushed in. "What's going on?"

I told her our news. B.J. started waltzing me around again. I laughed and laughed. B.J. put me down and I hugged Paige. "Oh, it's so wonderful, isn't it?"

She stared at me for a minute, and then my nine-year-old arched one brow and said, "Mother, don't you think this *might* be a little much."

That sent both of us into fresh gales of laughter.

With Nora's arrival, Paige began to deal with sharing her parents with a little stranger who demanded a lot of our energy. For the first time in Paige's life, we ran past her to say hello to someone else.

B.J. remained sensitive to Paige and talked to her often about our new status. After Dr. Keller called, confirming that I was 100 percent pregnant, we tried to help her adjust to the news of the second baby as well.

"Well, I suppose we can manage," she said in her grown-up tones.

Paige loved Nora and never showed resentment toward her. At the same time she had to share her busy parents a little more. When the new baby came, it would take even more maturity and understanding on our daughter's part.

The tensions between Paige and me had not gone away. I'm sure the addition of one new baby and another on the way didn't help matters. At times I could tell that Paige felt she was being elbowed out of the family. In those moments of awareness, both B.J. and I tried to reassure her.

"It's not that we love you less or them more," I said.

"They're tiny. They need a lot of attention," B.J. said. "Like you did when you were a baby."

She nodded and said she understood. Yet I sensed that underneath she felt quite insecure and pushed aside. I determined to be more sensitive to her needs and less demanding of her.

Paige's circumstances were drastically different from those of my own childhood. Yet, at the age of nine both of us felt we had nowhere to belong. I just couldn't understand how this could have happened to her. We loved Paige. We had tried so hard to show her that love.

She now had material security and no worries about where we'd live or if we would have enough to eat. Both B.J. and I loved her and showered her with affection. Despite our efforts, I continued to sense an emotional parallel between her childhood and mine. The thought terrified me. Why should this be? No one had cared about me. But we cared about Paige and told her often.

In a way I had been expecting this to happen, yet hoping it would not. B.J. and I had often talked about Paige's symptoms of withdrawal, moodiness, and passiveness as indicators of unresolved conflict dating from the early years of our marriage.

And when I saw Paige withdraw, I blamed myself. I had failed again.

"With another baby on the way, can we just go on like this?" I asked. "Maybe we need to get help for Paige."

"Or help for us," B.J. said.

"She's not quite ten now. I don't want her growing up confused and ending up in terrible emotional shape at nineteen," I said.

A friend recommended a psychologist, and we visited him. After four or five visits we found our anxiety level relieved a little. But we had not received any real help from him. He finally suggested that we postpone any further sessions until after the birth of Erin/Aaron.

"Good idea," B.J. said, knowing we were not getting anywhere.

"Yes," I said, knowing we wouldn't go back.

Somehow we knew we were close to finding the answers to our conflicts. We just weren't sure what to do.

By Christmas, I was five and a half months pregnant. We had plenty of things to occupy our minds. We decided to put Paige back in a regular school in January. Terry would remain on as a secretary until I had the baby in May.

By this time both of us just knew the baby would be a boy. We started referring to Aaron. B.J. and I attended the Lamaze natural childbirth classes.

We postponed searching for any new light on our problems until after the baby came.

15

Out of Control

A lot of things about the pregnancy with Aaron/Erin brought back the painful memories of my pregnancy with Paige. At that time, we lived in New York City and went through a tragic year. Paige was born during the success following "Raindrops."

Although I wanted a baby, I felt so trapped. I wasn't in control of my own life. And except for the period when I was recovering from an automobile accident at age seventeen, I had always been in control.

Control? Thinking back it seems strange to use that word. In those days, I not only lacked control, I couldn't even take care of myself.

B.J., experiencing the pressures of fame and success mixed with equal parts of drugs and confusion, hardly knew I existed.

From the second through the fourth months of my pregnancy, I was sick every day, all day long. In the latter months I developed toxemia. The fifth and sixth months were the only times I felt well during the entire pregnancy. Those two months were like an oasis for me in the desert of maddening confusion.

Had I known more about nutrition and physical fitness, I wouldn't have experienced such a difficult time, nor battled so much with personality changes. During all the bad months I hit emotional lows and felt suspicious of everyone. *Negative, fearful, insecure*—these words describe my worst moods. A loud noise would start me crying or screaming. I couldn't tolerate silence either.

I wanted to lean on B.J., but his drug problem, coupled with trying to perform each night, consumed all his energy. Even in my predicament, I was still in far better shape than B.J.

"I think I'm going crazy," I said to him one day.

He laughed it off.

I couldn't dismiss it so easily. I felt I was going over the edge. I've always been outgoing and known that I'd survive. But during my pregnancy something snapped inside, and I couldn't cope. I even doubted my survival.

Already in a state of depression, I felt utterly trapped. Even in the worst days of my childhood I had never felt so alone and helpless. Even then, I could find my way out of a problem.

But this time I saw no release. Each day was worse. Because of the nature of his profession, B.J. often had to leave New York, and I would be alone for five or six days at a time. I was scared to be alone.

I had no idea how to cope in a big city like New York. I didn't even know how to hail a taxi. I was afraid to ask anyone for directions.

I tried talking to B.J.'s manager or agent. They never saw me as a person. They treated me as someone to tolerate and deal with only when necessary. Mostly they saw me as property—like one of B.J.'s cars.

In my depression, I envisioned myself walking in a dark tunnel that had no way out. I was losing control—and that scared me. My mind would no longer function, and my reasoning became irrational.

I, who had always been a survivor, no longer cared about living. For the first time, I wanted to die.

B.J. had returned from a road trip then, exhausted and sleepless. I needed him so badly. I only wanted him to hold me, to say something comforting to me, or simply to kiss me on the cheek.

Instead B.J. hardly spoke as he walked like an eighty-year-old man into the bedroom. He collapsed on the bed, not even bothering to take off his shoes.

B.J. was working the Copacabana and was completely strung out on drugs.

I stood in the middle of the room several minutes, watching as he fell into a deep sleep. He had absolutely no idea of my pain. He didn't care. No one cared.

"No one cares whether I live or die," I said aloud. "I don't matter to anyone."

And it no longer mattered to me either.

I walked over to B.J.'s stash of drugs in the closet and took out enough Quaaludes to end my life. I lay down next to B.J. who had already passed out. He had been so high that day, and ordinarily once he fell asleep it would take him two days to regain consciousness.

But for some unexplained reason, B.J. woke up. He looked at me. A pasty foam covered the corners of my mouth. It was a kind of cruddy paste that is a reaction to drugs. Once a person has seen that chalky substance, it's unmistakable.

B.J. knew I never took drugs, and immediately he guessed what had happened. He called the rescue squad and tried to revive me.

I survived. More amazingly, Paige was born without any problems.

Later, I looked back and called that my "temporary insanity." My doctor confirmed that some women react that way during pregnancy. Within six weeks after Paige's birth, the majority of my symptoms had disappeared and I felt like the old Gloria again. I no longer felt trapped, and I sensed I was moving back into control again.

If anything, I felt stronger, knowing I could tackle the problems at hand. I also began to realize, for the first time, that I didn't have to stay with B.J. I could always take Paige and walk out. That thought had never occurred to me before.

During my second pregnancy I didn't have any symptoms of "temporary insanity" until a few weeks before the birth. And for several weeks afterward I went through what is called postpartum depression. In my case, it went much deeper than depression. This strange behavior showed up in all kinds of ways.

I picked on Bev, whom I'd never criticized before. "Can't you do anything right?" I screamed.

"I'm sorry, honestly, I—"

"I don't want excuses, and I don't want apologies. Just do what you're getting paid for."

"Yes, Ma'am," she said.

This went on day after day. Finally Bev took two weeks of vacation.

Under normal conditions, talking to Bev when I'm down lifts my spirits. She provides the most calming effect in my life. In our eight years together, during my second pregnancy was the only time we ever had problems.

I was afraid all the time, and my mind filled with every possible tragedy. What if robbers broke into the house when I was alone with Nora and Paige? What if B.J.'s plane crashed? Suppose I never recovered from this craziness and had to be put in some kind of institution?

I didn't try to tell most of these irrational fears to anyone for a long time. That made them even more tormenting. I called it controlled terror.

Finally I tried. "B.J., I'm terrified."

"What's troubling you?" he asked in his slow way of speaking.

"I'm scared. Scared to death."

"Of what?"

"Of everything. Of nothing. I'm just scared every moment."

"You look fine—"

"I may look fine, but that's all outward. Inside I'm terrified."

"About what?"

"Dozens of things. Hundreds. Like—like what if the baby's deformed? What if I slide over the edge and try suicide again? I'm afraid to walk into a room in the dark. I can't sleep because sometimes I'm afraid I won't wake up." My voice rushed on, giving him dozens of examples of my fears. Yet, even in my own confused mind I knew I sounded strange.

"You're going to be all right," he said, probably not knowing what else to say. And what could he do? What could anyone do?

"I—I don't know if I will or not . . ."

He held me. "Everything's going to be fine. You're just going to be a mama again, and you're thinking too much about the responsibility."

During my second "temporary insanity" I felt as though I were in a time warp. It threw me back to the emotional state of those days in New York. Only this time I could sit down and reason a little better. I also knew that my family and friends loved me. I had people around to help take care of my physical needs. The presence of others helped me begin to penetrate the cloud of mystery that I had never uncovered during those ten years between pregnancies.

Yet, even though I knew I was irrational, it didn't solve anything.

One day I started to tell Paige how to hang up a beautiful party dress. I stopped in mid-sentence, unable to remember what I was talking about.

Later I tried to explain to B.J. "It's like trying to stand on a foot that has gone to sleep. One minute I'm fine, the next I'm sprawling on the floor."

Other times, so Paige and B.J. later told me, I'd try to explain something and my words wouldn't make sense.

Sounds frightened me because they became distorted. Slight noises magnified themselves. Loud noises hardly distracted me.

Time and love, provided by my Lord, my family, and my friends, were the two main ingredients of the medicine that eventually got me back to my old self again. Nutrition information and exercise made the road to health available, and I eagerly read about both.

On June 4, 1979, Erin Micah was born by the Lamaze method. B.J. stayed with me and coached me through the delivery. I received only a mild painkiller in the delivery room.

I felt great and fed Erin in the recovery room. While other women were still in the recovery room, I had gone to my room, showered, and dressed. Two days later I went home.

Erin looked just like B.J., right down to the curly locks.

As I started to pull out of my depression, we tackled the challenge of straightening out our lives. We had realized our problems all during the ten years of our marriage, but had been emotionally too immature to tackle them in depth.

"We can't wait any longer," I said.

B.J. agreed.

"We're going to win over this monster that keeps threatening to destroy us and our relationship. We're going to win over all of this."

And as I said the words, somehow I knew we were going to win. I sensed we were closer to answers than ever before.

16

Forty Years in the Desert

We loved our infant and our toddler. Yet living with two diaper-clad babies every day meant we had to shift our life-style to fit their needs. Our lives became disorganized, and both B.J. and I needed time to adjust.

My emotional state confused Paige, even though I was pulling out of my depression. She saw my instability but did not have the maturity to grasp what had been happening. We sent her to camp in July, hoping that by the time she returned, we would have established a routine.

We didn't want Paige to feel left out of the family or that she stood in line behind Nora and Erin. So B.J. and I talked about one problem at a time. And the first problem was adjusting to two babies. Then I could work on establishing a closer relationship with Paige.

B.J. and I had not gotten into full harmony. Although our arguments were not as violent as in earlier years, it was only because we had learned how to restrain our anger. In spite of our Christian teaching, much prayer, and opening ourselves to God, we still felt we needed to become whole people.

Once we settled into our new routine, we decided we had to find a new counselor. Although our previous one had not been as helpful as we'd wanted, he had opened my eyes to a single truth.

I had been sitting across from his desk, telling him about all the anger and abusive language B.J. heaped on me.

"And you take it?" he said calmly.

I don't remember how I answered. I do know I decided that from that time on, our relationship would be different. Perhaps without realizing it, the counselor had given me the most powerful weapon of all to cope.

"I don't have to accept B.J.'s angry outbursts as my responsibilities," I said aloud to myself when I was alone. As I thought of our years together, I saw that he continually blamed me when things went wrong. *And I believed him.* I allowed myself to take blame for everything.

B.J. and I talked a lot about that statement. The counselor's question contradicted what many of our Christian friends had been pounding into my head.

"Gloria, you're responsible to make B.J. happy," one woman said every time I mentioned our problems.

"So when he gets angry and screams at me, what do I do?"

"Whatever he tells you to do," she answered. Always the same answer, although said in different words. "Just submit yourself to whatever he demands. In time he will realize his errors and straighten out."

"But what if he doesn't?"

"He will. God promises."

That answer always ended it. If I argued, it sounded as if I were arguing against God or didn't have faith. Trapped again.

B.J. didn't straighten out. And he still grew angry. I tried to submit. For over a year, I honestly tried to do everything he asked. I took blame and accepted his irrational statements.

One day I announced, "B.J., after today I will no longer be emotionally responsible for your outbursts. I will not feel responsible to provide you with answers as I've always tried to do."

We talked about that for a long time before we both agreed. Yet agreeing did not automatically solve anything. We found ourselves reverting to old patterns. However, we had made a decision—a right decision.

This new stand forced B.J. to face his own anger. He has since been learning to accept the cause and effect of his own actions.

The decision also forced me to look at myself and my relationship to my husband. It is one thing to lend a hand when a person needs it, but another when you feel lending the hand is your responsibility in the first place.

I realize that I cannot, nor can anyone else, change the psychological makeup of another person, even when that person is my husband or my child. Everyone is responsible for that change himself.

We had not developed the skills to find happiness, but we had made a breakthrough! We now acknowledged that we were not the *cause* of each other's problems. We learned marriage is a natural conflict relationship. When two individuals come together as one, conflict is a necessary element. Because of our differing backgrounds, we were programmed to clash.

"We both need to grow up," I said. "And we can."

For us, we saw only one direction to go—straight ahead.

B.J. said to me, "If I really believe that Jesus Christ tells me in His Word that everything always works out for my good, then I must believe that this process is going to be a joyful journey."

I marveled at the simplicity of his faith.

After we talked a long time he also said, "No matter how rough it gets, we have peace, hope, and happiness—things we never had before. We can do it."

"I know we can," I answered.

Even though we were now building our relationship, patching cracks and making the foundation strong, we were able to enjoy each other in the process.

No overnight miracle took place. For the first few months, that determination brought out our claws. We fought often. We tried to make rules for fair fighting, but it was such an emotionally explosive time that we settled for "all is fair in love and war."

In the reflective times, we sat down and talked about recent insights. We looked at our developments and tried to strengthen each other through encouraging words and prayer. Most of all, we assured each other of God's love at work in us and our love for each other.

Just before Erin's birth, B.J. released his manager and transferred his business to his agent. During that transfer we became aware of many transactions for the first time. That meant serious financial strains again.

For months after the manager left, bills kept coming in. While the manager received half of everything we made, he'd neglected to use that money to pay the bills for travel, hotels, car rental, equipment, and hundreds of other expense items.

We had let it happen again.

We could do nothing but accept the fact, recover what we could, and keep on going. But we were beginning to learn.

We felt a capable agent would operate in B.J.'s best interests. He booked B.J. and handled our financial deals. We let him do this because we needed as much time to ourselves as possible. We had to sort through years of confusion and chaos, and we couldn't do that and run the business.

We felt much like Moses, who spent forty years in the desert with the Lord, getting his act together. Getting our act together was clearly what B.J. and I tried to do. My pregnancy with Erin slowed us down. We had to adjust our schedule a little more with each new inch of my waistline.

Then, after Erin's birth, we decided B.J. would stay home for nine months. We often talked about how unusual it was for everyone to be home so much.

"Maybe the Lord's just giving us the chance to regroup," B.J. said. "And we need it."

"God always gives us what we need," B.J. said.

During those weeks we felt that if we could break away from the pressures of the music world, we could sort out other parts of our lives.

We didn't always talk about big emotional issues. Often our conversation centered on babies, the Lamaze method, anything Oriental, losing weight, or diapers.

We also made another decision: We needed a separation from relatives and friends.

I can't think of any harder decision we had to make. If we had been in a normal profession, it would have been all right. But we had so much publicity that we had no time to be private people. So during our schedule of baby crazies we decided to limit our time with people outside the five of us. While emotionally difficult, both of us felt we had made the right decision. At times we both felt like "Benedict Arnolds" to our families.

It had taken us ten years to cut ourselves off. We had to do it for our own sakes. We knew that once we had made the separation we could return to relationships on a different basis. We had to achieve stability in our own lives. We saw that getting away from family troubles and influences would help us make that change.

Yet every day I felt guilty. If it hadn't been for B.J.'s determination to stay with me on that decision, I would have given in. We prayed often, asking God to help us. And we didn't retreat.

In our therapy sessions we often talked about this emotional separation from our families. Our therapist encouraged us. "I think you'll find it helpful," he said.

During this time, we also began learning about nutrition. We recognized that many of our physical and emotional problems could be eliminated by proper maintenance of our God-made machines— our bodies. We discovered, for instance, that B.J. is hypoglycemic. That in itself explained some of his mood swings.

Both of us dieted, not only because of the weight I needed to lose, but for our health and to keep in shape. Exercise entered our lives. I used swimming as a primary source of emotional and physical well-being. I swam the same day that Erin was born, and it continues to be a way for me to work out my frustrations. Living in hot Texas weather allows me to use our pool from May through October. In the colder months, I have a portable trampoline that I bounce on.

When I came home from the hospital with Erin, my scales told me I had to lose forty pounds. I had gone from a size eight to a fourteen. I remember thinking how big the designer name looked across my back pocket.

Some days I felt as if I were training for combat. I devised a regimen that included calisthenics and breathing exercises, and I added lifting, tugging, pushing, shoving, along with my regular exercises of diapering and minor household tasks.

After my exercises I'd sit in a hot tub and relax fully. After that I was able to cope with stressful situations more easily. I felt happier and healthier. I was emerging from my deep depressions.

We both discovered that our nutrition and exercise have more to do with our emotional stability than we had ever guessed. I enrolled in an aerobic dance class, and it helped me develop and maintain a higher energy level.

In working together we decided that our lives have three parts—physical, emotional, and spiritual. We had to provide for the care of all three.

In the midst of our changes in routine and getting ourselves together, we had other problems to face.

For instance, the new workload overwhelmed Bev. When she first came to work for us, she had only Paige and me. Now, we lived in a big house, B.J. was with us, and we had two preschoolers.

Because of his career, I often had to accompany B.J. on the road. We faced the problem of not enough people to do everything. We couldn't add anything more to poor Bev's duties.

At first, families from our church came in and stayed with the children. We knew that would only work temporarily, and we had to find a permanent solution.

I arranged schedules so that I never stayed away longer than two days at a time. But I still had to be away.

When Paige was an only child, she could stay with her grandmother or with a friend for a few days. Now we had three children, and we had to have a permanent baby-sitter. But that sitter also had to be someone the children would love.

We began praying for the Lord to send us someone.

I called a placement agency and through them hired a fifty-year-old woman to live in. It cost twice as much as I had planned to spend, but as B.J. said, "Honey, if it works out, it's worth the money."

"I know. The kids need someone around all the time."

Yet, even as I said those words, I knew we would have problems with the woman. I was starting to learn right at the beginning of a relationship when people weren't right for us.

Unfortunately, instead of facing the fact that it wouldn't work out, I went the other way. Systematically, in the same way I related to my own family during my childhood, the more unqualified I saw she was, the harder I tried to work things out. I was still "Miss-Fix-It-All-Up."

Without realizing it (and understanding it only in retrospect), I tried to mold that woman so that she could provide the type of responsible caring that I would like to have had from my own mother when I was young.

Because of all that, what should have been a simple decision to dismiss her proved difficult. I kept trying to make her fit.

The climax came when B.J. and I took an eight-day trip to Saudi Arabia, our longest time away from the children. When we returned, both babies were sick.

More than that, Bev quietly told us of the woman's neglect. Paige confirmed everything. For several nights I could hardly sleep, thinking about the way my three children had been treated.

Finally, I faced the woman. "I'm letting you go."

"Letting me go?" she asked, surprise written all over her face. "Why? Don't you like my work?"

"We're making other arrangements," I said, still the coward.

She started to argue, and I almost got caught in defending my position. Back to the old trap again. This time I sidestepped the danger. "I said we're making other arrangements," I said and left the room.

I felt guilty, cowardly, and angry at myself. But I also knew that I had learned how to avoid the buried mines in the battlefield and I had won a minor victory.

The day she left, in midwinter, she slipped on ice outside our front door and broke her leg. She sued us. Even so, we were rid of her.

During the two weeks the children were recuperating from infections, I had time to think and look deeply at myself. I was beginning to get a handle on the psychological game I played with myself.

"Always rescuing people, aren't you?" I asked my reflection in the mirror one day.

"Yes, I am," I answered back.

"Always picking up the pieces when someone fails to show responsibility. That's your pattern, isn't it?"

"Yes."

"Well? What are you going to do about it?"

I thought for a long time before I stared into the dark eyes of my reflection. "That's the hard part. Right now I know the kind of games I've played all my life. But I don't know yet how to change them."

"You'll find out," I heard myself answer.

And I knew I had spoken rightly.

I also knew that God would help me.

17

Growing Hurts

The search for a housekeeper began again. Wearily I wrote out a newspaper ad and, after a dozen changes, put it in four newspapers in the Dallas–Fort Worth area.

The responses came. I must have interviewed fifty applicants. This time I listened carefully to myself and to the applicants. I would not make another mistake by hiring the wrong person.

While I couldn't yet put it into words, on a subconscious level I was beginning to learn how to hire people, look for needed qualities, and quickly sense potential conflicts.

Lord, I prayed after all that interviewing, *if the next applicant I interview isn't right, then don't let me get any more people applying.*

The next one was unqualified.

For the next week, not a single letter came. I felt God had answered my prayer. But I still didn't have a housekeeper.

I changed the ad, and this time I mentioned not only housekeeping but also child care. I placed an ad in only one newspaper. "God can work as well through one ad as He can four," I told B.J.

I left a telephone number, and the first response came from a woman, obviously not an American.

"I've answered the ad," she said, "because it says you want someone to take care of children as well as keep house."

Her voice had a lilting sound to it. I tried to imagine what she looked like, because even over the phone, I knew I had found her.

Freida is a native of Ghana, West Africa. Her appearance almost staggered me. She is five-feet-six and large-framed. Her happy, round face and cheeks, coupled with a skin so dark it shone, fascinated me. I love the musical cadence to her voice.

After a short interview, I hired her. She returned for work the next day. Freida fit in immediately. We all loved this warm and sensitive person. She cooked everything in an original but delicious way.

At the end of her first day, I sat on the sofa several minutes thanking God for sending Freida to us. She was an answer to prayer, and I never doubted it.

Slowly B.J. and I moved together toward maturity. Battles still came up, and our tempers flared almost as much as before. Only our words now had less sting to them. We sensed that we still acted like caged animals charging the person who opened the door. But at least we were learning to control our anger. The Lord helped us in this through Bible reading and the teachings of great Christians.

It was during this period of time we heard that Francis Schaeffer would appear in Dallas for a seminar. We had seen the film series *Whatever Happened to the Human Race?* and we decided to attend the seminar.

We enjoyed listening to Dr. Schaeffer. He emphasized the principles of healthy living that we were beginning to grapple with.

We walked out of the seminar at lunchtime, feeling many new lights were being turned on in our heads. We talked about those new insights as we left the building.

Over lunch, somehow, we got back into one of our communication impasses. I closed my eyes, screaming inside. *God, how can this be? We were so enriched this morning, and now we're back in the same old battlefield again?*

B.J. took my hand, "Let's call off the fight for now."

"Okay," I agreed.

"Where did we go wrong this time?" he asked.

Even that was a new step for us. We had never been able to stop in the midst of a battle and analyze. All the other times we had to wait until both of us had cooled down. By then, we had forgotten what started it.

"I don't know, B.J. But we've got to start figuring it out *before* it happens."

We had several exchanges before B.J. stopped in mid-sentence. He put his hands on his hips and stared at me. "It's easy to figure out, Gloria. You just do what I tell you."

"What? Just like that?"

"Yes."

"Just because you say so?"

"All you have to do is shut your mouth and walk across the parking lot."

We stood about ten feet apart, looking as if we could be talking about steel-radial tires on the parked cars nearby. B.J. didn't raise his voice.

I replied in just as even a voice. "You have two options to draw on, B.J. You can either divorce me, or you can drag me across the parking lot. But I'm not going to walk over there just because you tell me."

We argued in those calm voices several more minutes, and I said, for the first time slightly raising my voice, "Not one more time, B.J. Thomas. Not one more time do I become a punching bag for your anger! You hit me and I'll punch you out or die trying. You yell at me and I'll give you a louder yell than you've ever heard before in your entire life!"

At that moment, in the midst of an argument, something flashed inside me. I grasped what the Bible means about maturity. God gives all of us moments of insight. But that's not enough. We have to take those insights and put them into practice.

For months B.J. and I had grasped truths about Christian maturity. We had been slow at making them realities.

Standing in the parking lot, ten feet apart, neither giving in to the other, I thought about Christian growth.

"B.J., you know we have a lot of knowledge. We know what the finished product will look like. But we haven't gone through the cleaning-up process yet."

"What?"

In spite of our argument, I laughed. My mind had been traveling on with the insight I had received, and poor B.J. had no idea what I was talking about. I explained.

He listened and then said quietly, "Let's just call a truce and go back for the afternoon seminar."

At the afternoon break, we ran into a pastor we both knew and arranged to eat together that evening. During the meal we kept our talk light. Finally B.J. said to the pastor, "We need help."

"What kind of help?"

"Someone we can talk to and who can understand our situation."

"I'll do what I can," he said.

We told him several things, and then the incident in the parking lot tumbled out.

"It was your duty, Gloria," he said looking straight at me. "You should have obeyed."

"What?" I asked absolutely amazed. "You mean just because he gets mad and tells me to walk across a parking lot, I'm to do it?"

"That's right," he answered.

"I've been hearing this for months," I said, "but somehow it just isn't right to me. Don't I have any rights?"

"You see, Gloria, your duty to God is to obey B.J. If you're faithful, God will soften B.J.'s heart so that he won't give you irrational commands."

I sat there, stunned, not knowing how to reply. Everything within me said the pastor was wrong. But I had no idea of how to answer him. In that confusing atmosphere, I remembered that counselor who had talked to me about each person being responsible for his or her own actions.

As the pastor and B.J. both spoke to me about obedience, I kept remembering the time the counselor had said, "And you take that?"

Again and again those words buzzed through my brain. I opened my mouth to explain, and the pastor assumed I wanted to argue. He leaned forward. "Gloria, all you have to do is yield yourself to your husband. It's that simple."

"I—I can't," I said.

"You must."

After conflicts with B.J. I often felt humiliated or saw myself as a total failure. I was sliding into that position again.

I would have, too, except that counselor's question kept troubling me. *And you take that?*

In Manila I had begun to grasp truths to deliver us from our dysfunctional living skills. Again in Israel, everything got clearer. Now I realized that those insights had borne fruit. I saw the old patterns, *as they were recurring.*

I felt humiliated and a failure because I *chose* to become a victim. I kept allowing the situation to get so out of control that I forced B.J. into making irrational demands, and then I defied him. No wonder we couldn't resolve our conflicts.

It all seemed so clear to me. When two people love each other and want the other's happiness, they don't get caught up in the authority conflict. They each work for the other's happiness. The questions of authority and submission come only in the midst of conflict. And conflict comes when one or both is defensive, angry, or not acting totally out of love.

I burst out with, "Wait a minute, you don't understand—"

I never had a chance to say anything more. For at least the fourth time I heard the same lecture about joyfully submitting myself to the head of the household.

Suddenly, my tears started flowing, and I couldn't stop them. I was sorry for the squabble. Sorry for hundreds of fights over the years. Sorry it had taken so long to understand such simple things about living. I couldn't explain all that to the pastor and B.J. I could only cry.

A woman approached our table. "Mr. Thomas, may I have your autograph?"

"Of course," B.J. said, accepting a seminar bulletin and pen. He signed his name, smiled at the woman, and all the time, I sat at the table crying softly. Two or three other people came up, asking for autographs. No one seemed to notice my tears.

Finally I calmed down. "Let me explain," I said and tried to tell them of my sudden insight. They didn't listen. Or perhaps I explained poorly. I only know that after every second sentence they interrupted, and I felt bulldozed by the advice I kept getting.

I stopped talking and the incident passed.

"Well, let's go back to the seminar," B.J. said.

A friend had made arrangements for us to meet the Schaeffers after the evening seminar. B.J. sensed we had not resolved our immediate conflict. He had no idea what to do, but he knew we were still at odds. He sent word that he couldn't meet with the Schaeffers, and we headed straight home.

We sat in the living room, trying to look objectively at what had happened. B.J.'s eyes clouded with tears, making me know he hated the incident as much as I did.

There are times when each of us feels the other mate is responsible for a particular conflict, making us feel more self-righteous in our position. In this situation, however, both B.J. and I felt awful. He said the words he had been taught by family training and he felt they were right.

"B.J., I'm sorry I haven't been submitting . . ." I couldn't finish. The tears started again. But more than the tears stopping me, I no longer believed what had been drummed into my head for the past two years.

I jumped up and moved several feet away. "I want to do what you tell me. I want to say the words you're asking me to say. But I can't do it—not that way."

"Gloria, I don't know who's wrong in all of this. But, honey, we can't give up."

"Give up? Who's talking about giving up?" I said as I came back and put my arm around him.

B.J. and I talked for a long time, and he held me close. We expressed our love for each other. We were more committed than ever.

I knew we had passed another milestone in our relationship. We were getting more in tune. We had begun to recognize the problems as they occurred. Soon, we would be able to anticipate them. And by anticipating, we could prevent the conflicts.

"Growing sure hurts," I said. "It hurts a lot."

"But it's worth it," B.J. answered.

18

Taking the Reins

"Come quickly! Come quickly!" Freida cried out.

I was taking a shower. Freida had never come into my bedroom before without knocking first. This time she burst in, her breath short, and her eyes anxious. "Come quickly," she said in her lilting way.

"Something terrible has happened to one of the children!" I shrieked. I didn't even dry off but threw on my housecoat and prayed as I ran after her, *O Lord, please, Lord!*

As I ran down the stairs, I saw Erin and Nora playing on the floor. I paused long enough to say, "Thank You, God."

Freida threw open the front door. I saw a sign posted in our yard. I ran outside and read the words. The Internal Revenue Service had put it up, declaring that our house was up for public auction.

My ears started ringing, my lips went numb, and I felt an electric current shooting through my arms. "Oh!"

I hurried back inside the house, I walked calmly upstairs to my bedroom, and then I wept.

Money management had always been a problem. Our accounts would be bulging with money, yet the people who took care of our business did their work so poorly that they overlooked details, like paying bills on time. Once the bank repossessed our car, taking it from the driveway in the middle of the night. More than once they had repossessed other items. They had always done their work quietly and privately.

But that sign declared to the whole world that we had financial problems. My brain kept saying, *It can't be! It can't be!*

The sign was real.

"We've been paying the IRS right along. Just the way we agreed!"

I called our agent and started checking. The current agent, we discovered, was disorganized, started projects that he never finished, negotiated deals and then never got around to signing contracts. He had done that with the IRS. They had sent him papers that should have been completed and returned. He had not done the paperwork. The IRS, feeling they had no other option, declared our house up for auction.

After several frantic calls, I talked to a higher-up in the IRS who had power to rescind the order. They agreed to take down the sign, and we promised to fill out the papers immediately.

B.J. and I called our attorneys, agents, and manager. We were expecting several large royalty checks within the next six to eight weeks. We arranged for our attorney to receive the money and transfer it directly to the IRS. The accountant said he would work on the forms the IRS sent and would also make sure we had all our figures straight. The agent agreed to work directly with the IRS to forestall any future happenings like their putting up an auction sign again.

At last I felt relief, everyone buzzed around with enough energy to build a bridge in their spare time, and we forgot about the matter.

One morning, nearly two months later, Freida came to my room and knocked softly. "Please, you need to come now."

Although she spoke gently, her face told me something was definitely wrong. She led me downstairs to the front door.

It had happened again—an auction notice.

I rushed back in the house, called the IRS, only to learn that our agent, lawyer, and accountant had not completed the work they had agreed to do. Inside I fumed and some of it spilled over on the phone. The IRS gave us four days to straighten out the tangles and to keep the notice out of the local papers.

We arranged for the IRS to pick up the royalty check already in the lawyer's office. We met the four-day deadline.

B.J. and I didn't want any public knowledge about this. But we had gone through so much in the past years, it was only one more crisis. Yet we did care. Wire services often picked up this kind of information about public figures. Once negative press gets out, it's difficult on family members and on friends. The children suffer, too, because of their classmates.

"There's so much uncertainty about our way of life," B.J. said during this particular time.

"Uncertainty?" I remember answering. "It's like walking across the room, suspecting nothing, while all the time someone is hiding in the corner, ready to pull that rug out from under you."

The uncertainty of our business system kept me under constant tension. We paid our employees well, and yet we found nothing but errors, and we were always just one step from chaos.

B.J. and I sat down and talked about our business affairs.

We tried everything to avoid getting into the business process itself. "We're just too busy."

I felt it was too complicated for me to handle. My favorite excuse went like this: "We don't have enough energy to work at changing ourselves and still give the business a fair shake."

We couldn't continue copping out. B.J. and I were making progress in our relationship. Now we had to face the other issues of daily living.

Both of us had been chronically naive. We finally reached the place where we could no longer blame naiveté. We sat down and evaluated where we had come from, where we were now, and where we were headed in B.J.'s career.

"B., I can't work on where we're headed until we both know where we've come from."

"We've been looking at ourselves since we became Christians," he said.

He was right. We had to move on. B.J. suggested again that I take over the business.

I already knew the next step. "Look, B.," I said, "if we keep close touch with what's going on and I supervise the whole operation, I can't see that it will cause any more problems than we already have."

B.J. knew it would get complicated, but it was his idea from the beginning that I get involved.

"Can it be worse than having our whole business blow up every six months?"

"What you're suggesting might solve a few problems before they happen."

"Then let's try it," I said, sounding more confident than I felt.

"Where do we begin?" B.J. asked, as overwhelmed as I.

After a long discussion, we decided to hire a secretary to take care of the routine office things such as answering the phone and correspondence. We would not touch any deals already in progress, but as each project came up, more and more of the work would come to me personally.

It sounded simple in our conversation. What a surprise I had coming! Accounts were six months behind.

"Yeah, but it's still in better shape than it's been in before," B.J. reminded me, as I tried to fight my way through piles of papers and legal documents.

It embarrassed me that we constantly received a rash of unpaid travel bills. We had always insisted that those expenses came first.

"I can't understand this," I said, waving a sheaf of bills at our manager. "We always make sure everything is accounted for after each road trip. Everything—down to the last dollar."

"And travel expenses get taken care of first," B.J. reminded him.

"Just sorta got behind," he said sheepishly.

"We won't get behind again," I said. I still didn't know a lot about the business, but I had a good head and I would learn. I got quite an education. The business end involved more than contracting for B.J. to give a concert or make a TV appearance. We also faced things like travel arrangements for each of the seven band members, all living in different cities. We had publicity to think of, contracts, sleeping accommodations, and sound equipment. It seemed as if we had fifty specific things to do every time B.J. sang publicly.

"I'm going to learn," I vowed. "And once I've learned, we're going to have the best system in the music business." I also knew that, with God's help, we could do it.

It took us months to fully understand the system. But once we figured it out, analyzed more efficient ways of handling things, and asked ourselves, "How can we make it better?" things turned around.

We're proud of the way we handle business now. We leave nothing to chance and know exactly what, when, and how things should be done. This smooth operation makes it easier for B.J. to perform, because he doesn't worry about last-minute details or wonder if someone has forgotten anything.

When they inducted B.J. into the Grand Ole Opry Hall of Fame as their sixtieth member, we made sure that the media knew of the event. We got as much publicity out of that occasion as possible. A number of people in the business commented on how smoothly everything went.

"You folks really know what you're doing," an old hand in Nashville said to me.

He didn't realize what a compliment he was paying us.

Mr. and Mrs. Vernon Thomas
—B.J.'s parents. *Below:* The
Vernon Thomas family. *Left
to right:* Geneva, Vernon,
Judy, Billy Joe, Jerry.

Billy Joe, Vernon, and Jerry. *Left:* Gloria's family. *Clockwise from left:* Gloria, Harold, Louise, and Harry Richardson.

Gloria, Harry, Louise holding Tracy, Harold holding Joyce. *Left:* Gloria, 1954, in Doonis, Virginia.

Gloria, 1956.

B.J. at the Long Island
Arena, 1966.

Jerry and B.J. on the road. *Below:* B.J. and Kenny Rogers, 1971.

Gloria, 1963.

Gloria's senior portrait, 1967.

Mr. and Mrs. B.J. Thomas, December 9, 1968, Chapel of the Bells, Las Vegas, Nevada.

B.J. and Gloria with Paige, New York City, 1970. *Left:* Gloria and Paige, 1975.

Gloria's writing press photo, 1977. (Photo by Frank Munson.)

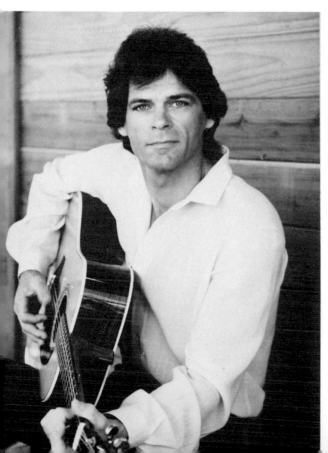

B.J., 1978. (Photo by Frank Munson.)

B.J.'s band. *Left to right:* Pat Vines, Larry Chavis, Steve Hodge, John Francis, and Danny Young. Not pictured—Carl Greeson. *Below:* B.J., Paige, and Gloria in Capernaum.

The first picture B.J. saw of
Park Soo Mee (Nora) as he sat
at the kitchen table. *Below:*
Nora Lam Sung, Park Soo
Mee, Gloria, and Paige.

B.J. and Paige, 1980. B.J. and Nora, 1980. *Below:* Freida Kudiabor holding Erin, Paige, and Bev Mitchell holding Nora, 1980.

Gloria, 1980. (Photo by Frank Munson.) *Below:* Dr. Robert H. Schuller, Gloria, and B.J., 1980.

RainSong Management Company. *Left to right:* Janet Kelly, B.J., and Gloria. (Photo by Frank Munson.) *Below:* B.J., Nora, Paige, Gloria, and Erin, 1980. (Photo by Frank Munson.) Erin, 1981. (Photo by Frank Munson.)

Billy Graham's Las Vegas
Crusade, 1981. *Left to right:*
B.J., June and Johnny Cash,
Billy Graham, and Bev Shea.
Right: Roy Acuff and Gloria
at the Grand Ole Opry, 1981.

B.J. becomes the sixtieth member of the Grand Ole Opry on August 7, 1981—his thirty-ninth birthday. *Left to right:* Pete Drake, Gloria, Joel Katz, Rose Trimble, and B.J. *Left:* B.J.'s golf swing.

19

Losers Always Lose

So far this book has been our story through Gloria's eyes. In these next four chapters I want to tell the story from my perspective.

As Gloria has pointed out in earlier chapters, we were products of our backgrounds. We could not make any significant changes until we saw *who* we were and *why* we acted and reacted the way we did.

I was born Billy Joe Thomas in Hugo, Oklahoma, on August 7, 1942, the second child in the family. Jerry was eighteen months older, and Judy came along nearly eight years later.

The best way to write about my early life would be to tell you about my dad, Vernon Thomas. He was one of four children, and his father operated a corn-liquor still in the woods around Corsicana, Texas. His father drank a lot, and my dad drove him around most of the time.

Because he was around the corn liquor and a father who drank heavily, it is easy to understand why by the time my dad was thirteen, many considered him an alcoholic. As he grew older, he earned a reputation for being the "biggest hell raiser in the farming communities of East Texas," as one relative said.

My father met Geneva Talbot, fell in love, and wanted to marry her. Her parents opposed the marriage. Instead of stopping Vernon Thomas, that only encouraged him to thwart them. One night they went on a date—and decided to get married. Four years later, Geneva gave birth to Jerry.

I don't remember a lot about what happened before I went to

school. My father had a good job working in air conditioning. He was also a contractor, but he liked the air conditioning better. "Helps me work up a good sweat," he'd say.

Dad never sat still, always needing to be in motion. That's one reason he got into the occupation he did; he never liked to stay indoors.

Dad probably would have made a good living for us, and we would have grown up a typical, middle-class Texas family—except for one real problem: Dad couldn't stay in one place. He moved all the time. Besides having troubles caused by his drinking, he always thought he could find a better job in a different town. We just didn't have any real roots anywhere, except to say we lived in Texas.

Things were bad for the family most of the time. I don't remember much, mostly what Mom or Dad told me as I grew up. I do remember that besides Dad's problem, Jerry had one too. He developed polio when I was about four years old. Jerry pulled out of the polio all right, but it left him with a hearing problem.

Jerry had a strong spirit and compensated for his handicap by being "Mr. Tough Guy." For him, it was a way to survive with dignity. He didn't want pity; he only wanted acceptance. He became the "James Dean" rebel of his time. And for Jerry, during those growing-up years, I guess it was the only way he could survive.

My mother, I realize now as I look back, probably had the hardest time of all. When I was small, she tried to stand up to Dad.

"Vernon, we're happy here. You'll find a good job soon," she said once when Dad announced another move.

"I've heard there's a lot of work over near Houston."

"But the kids. They've been moved around so many times."

"I've made up my mind. We're going!"

We moved that time. We moved every time Dad felt the itch to try a new place or get a better job.

Mom did her best for us. She tried to protect us and make us feel loved. We didn't have much discipline at home. We learned early that if we wanted something, we asked Mom.

Mom took care of us. She'd complain now and then that we didn't pick up clothes or put away toys, but she always did everything for us.

I remember one time Dad left for work saying, "Boys," meaning mostly me, "I want the yard mowed by the time I get back this evening." Dad didn't threaten. He didn't have to; we knew what he meant.

We went on to school—it was almost the end of the school year. When we got home, Jerry and I started fighting about the grass.

"I did it last time," I said, "and I'm not going to do it again!"

"I did it! And last year I did it alone almost all summer!" Jerry threw back at me.

We squabbled, argued, and yelled. Finally Mom went out and mowed the grass herself.

At the time, both Jerry and I felt relieved. We had gotten her to do it for us. Only years later, after we had grown up, would we realize that it prevented our learning to face responsibility for ourselves. But during those growing-up years I avoided responsibility.

I wasn't happy, however, during my childhood. Mainly because my parents didn't know how to express love. I never thought they really loved me. My immature reasoning said they loved Jerry because of his handicaps. They loved Judy because she was a girl. They had no reason to love me. In reality, my dad didn't know how to express love to anyone.

I suffered from low self-esteem (although I didn't know words like that then). I also felt somehow responsible for the fact that we always fought and yelled at each other.

That's how we usually settled anything at home. We screamed, yelled, or punched each other—whatever it took—until someone won. Dad, being bigger and stronger, usually won, and Mom always gave in.

We had no discipline, no family unity, but mostly no love. And, like all humans, I wanted to be loved. Gloria once said to me, "B.J., one reason you sing the sad songs so meaningfully is because you know the pain that those songs express."

Maybe I do.

I needed affection and I didn't get it at home. I tried getting that kind of love and attention from my grandfather. I often spent my summers with him.

One time I said, "Grandpa, sometimes I think you pay attention to Jerry all the time, but you never do to me. Do you love Jerry more than you do me?"

Grandpa stared at me and said, "Boy, you don't have the right to ask that question." Then he walked away.

In my immature mind, I could only believe he meant that he actually did love Jerry more. Everybody loved Jerry more. Or so it seemed to me. I felt only that no one loved me. That's what hurt the most. I went through my growing-up years always assuming I wasn't any good, not worth loving.

As Gloria put it, our family structure functioned like a punctured tire. One side was always flat. We never functioned like a normal family. We couldn't—we didn't know how.

In those days, no matter how hard I tried, I couldn't please Dad. I now realize that no one could have pleased him. Mom never had a chance. Nothing she ever said seemed right to Dad, and he would say to her, "Geneva, just shut your stupid mouth."

Sometimes he'd slap her across the face, saying, "I don't need some dumb woman telling me what to do."

The worst times came about when Dad drank—which was often. He'd break things, and after every second word he'd insert a string of curses.

In his own way, Dad was trying to be loved and didn't know how. Sometimes during his rampages, Mom would finally stand up to him and get hit for her trouble. It seemed useless for anyone to oppose him.

Later, when Dad passed out drunk on the sofa, she'd say to us, "Your dad's been drinking, and he doesn't mean what he says. He doesn't even know what he's doing when he slaps you."

He constantly yelled at me, things like "You shiftless, lazy, worthless no-good son." *Lazy* was his favorite word. It never occurred to me that the things he screamed at me weren't true. So I grew up believing I was lazy. When I went to school I figured the other kids knew I was lazy.

If someone had only helped me realize during those growing-up years that just because my father yelled at me, cursed me, and called me lazy, didn't make it true. But I had no way of knowing differently. He was my dad, and I believed him.

We were always poor. The times when Dad drank heavily, we would get to the point where we had nothing left to eat. Then he'd lose his job. He'd complain because we ate so much or threw away good food. He always found something to complain about.

I do remember one bright spot. I had joined a Little League team. That year we won the championship, and everyone said I was the best player on the team. That meant a lot to me—it was one of the few really good things that happened in my childhood.

We moved around so much that we didn't have many friends, but that summer I got close to the other players. We visited each other's homes a lot. I always stayed with them as long as I could. Their houses were filled with a feeling of "home" and a sense of peace. And also, I didn't like going home.

One of the guys found out that we hadn't had any meat for at least two weeks. His parents owned a butcher shop, and every week for a long time they would bring us nice cuts of meat—better cuts than we ever bought for ourselves.

I liked the food, but it embarrassed me. We had been poor a long time, but we had never taken charity. Dad always said he took care of his family and didn't need any outside interference.

I just kept wishing Dad would go back to work and then they would stop giving us meat all the time.

I used to think, *If he'd just stop drinking and sober up, he could go back to work.* I didn't realize then—and didn't until I had gone through my own problem with drugs—that you can't just "sober up." Dad was sick—and I didn't realize how sick. He died when I was twenty-nine years old, before I'd handled my own problems.

All through life I wanted Dad to love me, and I didn't feel he ever did. He absolutely didn't know how to love.

The only way my dad ever showed any affection was that once in a while he'd start playing with us. He'd grab me and tickle me or pinch me. At first it was fun, but he wouldn't stop. He'd punch me on the arm or pinch me so that it hurt.

Some nights when I went to bed, I'd hear my dad screaming and shouting. He'd get Jerry or Judy, or sometimes even Mom. He'd have them laughing, then crying, and finally I'd hear him slapping them. It scared me, and I would lie in the dark a long time, wondering if life would always be so awful.

Dad smoked two packs of cigarettes a day. He was always burning holes in the furniture, because he'd pass out with one still lit. Often I'd sneak in after he quieted down and check on him. More than once I put out a cigarette that might have set the bed on fire.

Dad also took a lot of medicines. He complained about pains in his head and back. He kept his dresser and the bathroom filled with remedies, painkillers, and medications. I worried about his health.

I really wanted Dad to love me. I tried in every way I knew to get him to love me. Looking back, it seems crazy the things I did. I'd break a glass or fall down and hurt myself. Anything, I suppose, to get him to notice me. But, other than a few yells or a slap on the side of the face, Dad never did seem to respond.

As I grew up I felt alone and unloved, and I blamed myself for it. My friends talked about their fathers taking them places. Others said their dads bought a record player and records and even taught them how to dance. Some went camping or fishing. Nothing like that ever went on in our home.

At times I hated my father, and yet I idolized him, too. And, as sick as he was, I made up my mind to be like him.

I envisioned my dad as a cross between Humphrey Bogart and Robert Taylor. When he was drinking, he acted like tough-guy Bogart. When sober, he had the suave, self-assured presence of Robert Taylor.

Although I knew Dad didn't love me, I really didn't have as bad a time of it as Jerry did. The two of them always had a fight going, as long as I can remember.

After Jerry's bout with polio, Dad treated him as if it had been Jerry's fault. He slapped him a lot and yelled at him constantly. I remember one time when Dad kept telling Jerry, "Get that hair cut. You look like some girl."

Jerry, more to please Dad than anything, finally had his hair cut.

When Dad came home, Jerry went up to him. "Dad, what do you think about my haircut?"

"It looks like hell."

The smile disappeared from Jerry's face. He stood there and cried. Jerry didn't cry often, and I never again saw him cry in front of Dad.

When Jerry and I were still young we made a promise to each other—we would always be best friends. And as I look at my life and the people around me, Jerry is still here. He's the best friend I have in the whole world. And for a lot of those rough years, it was just Jerry and me against the whole world.

One time I asked, "Dad, why are things this way? We don't have things like other families, and we're always fighting."

"Billy," he said, "I guess you just weren't meant to make it in this life."

I didn't say anything. I was afraid to, but in my mind I thought, *Yeah, you ought to know.*

Over and over as I grew up, I heard the same message—I wasn't meant to make it in this life. Not that I actually heard those words. But our whole way of life kept giving me the message that I wasn't any good and I would never make anything out of myself.

This became clear to me at one baseball game. I was a good player and usually better than most of the others. In that particular game, we had two outs, and the team was depending on me to win the game. I saw the ball coming toward me, but I just couldn't lift that bat off my shoulder. I saw the balls coming, and ordinarily I could have hit any of them, but not that time.

We lost the game. I took the whole burden, thinking that I had lost the game for the team. But then, what else could I expect?

After the game my mom said, "That's okay, Billy."

Dad didn't say anything. But the look on his face seemed to say, "Well, what else did you expect? Losers always lose."

During the sixth grade I attended a Baptist church in Pasadena, Texas. We lived next to the church so it was the natural one to attend. I liked going there. It was my first refuge from a confusing home, and the people treated me well.

One Sunday the pastor gave an invitation to accept Jesus Christ as Savior. I didn't understand it all, but I went forward. People prayed for me and told me that I had been born again.

Later I rushed home and burst into the house, "Mama! I got born again today!"

Mama said, "Oh," as though embarrassed.

I stood in the middle of the room, suddenly feeling as if I had done something wrong. She said nothing more, and I walked away.

I went back to the church a few times, and not long after that, we moved away.

Each year the pattern always seemed the same. I'd begin to get involved with baseball or a church and then we'd move. As I grew older, I began learning to hide my emotions, too, especially from my dad. Nobody cared about me. Why should they? I wasn't worth anything anyway.

I probably would have remained a loser all my life except that God laid a hand on my shoulder. From that time in sixth grade, I've always known I belonged to God. But it would take another twenty years before I let Him lead my life.

20

Hank, Elvis, and B.J.

I saw Hank Williams only one time in my life. When I was in the third grade, Dad took the entire family to the Grand Ole Opry performance in Houston to see Hank Williams on the stage. He fell down on his knees, played the guitar, and sang.

As young as I was, I remember seeing the veins standing out on his neck—and I was sitting all the way in the balcony. I had never seen anybody sing like that—a person who absolutely threw himself into the song. I felt he meant every word he sang.

Later I made my Aunt Bonnie write down the words to "Setting the Woods on Fire." I memorized them and sang that song for years. I can still remember most of the words today.

Apparently I had musical talent—and so did my dad. But people like us never thought much about professional singing. I knew I could carry a tune but never thought there was anything unusual about me. Even if someone had told me I had a special musical gift, I probably wouldn't have believed it. I would more than likely have believed it if someone had said, "Billy, you sing terrible."

Dad sang mostly when he came home drunk. He especially liked the Hank Thompson song, "Hey Bartender Give Me One More and a Six-Pack for the Road."

I suppose that's the one thing my dad did for me—made me love music—and he didn't even realize he did that. Because Dad liked music, and especially country and western, I listened to that kind of music a lot.

I had just reached my teens when I heard the man who I still think had the greatest singing voice America has ever heard in popular music—Elvis Presley.

I bought Elvis's first album, and one song, "Old Shep," really touched me. I must have sung that song a thousand times around the house. That was all part of my training, but I didn't know that then.

I do know that singing became the one way I could let myself go. When I sang, even when I began to perform publicly, I put myself totally into the song. I *felt* the music. The words came from my guts.

Even today when I sing, I try to do more than entertain. I search for songs I can relate to. When a song speaks to me, then I know it can speak to others as well.

Maybe I don't know all the heartbreak I sing about in specific songs, but I've known enough pain and rejection so that I can identify with almost every kind of sorrow. I've also known a lot of joy. In the early days, most of that good feeling was drug-induced. But in more recent years, I've known those highs through God's love and through the good relationship Gloria and I have built together.

But that came later. In my teen years I sang for me. I never thought of professional singing. Once in a while I'd have a nice fantasy. I'd sing along with an Elvis record or harmonize with Hank Williams. I'd close my eyes, imagining myself on a stage singing for thousands. But those were daydreams like most people have at various times.

The real move toward professional singing came about almost by accident—at least I saw it that way at the time. Jerry and I had drifted apart. He ran around with a rough group who fought and drank a lot. On the other hand, I played baseball and still had the idea of being a clean-cut, all-American boy. But when I was fifteen I had a bad year. Our team lost fourteen games straight. The coach took me out after the eighth game, and I sat on the bench for the next six. I decided I was a loser in baseball too and would never play again.

About that time, people stopped calling me Billy and I became B.J., because we had so many Bills on the baseball teams I played with. Then, when I started singing professionally, a local talent whose first name was Billy Joe was creating a lot of interest. So from then on, everyone called me B.J.

I drifted that summer and got in with a rough crowd who smoked and drank. They fought a lot. And, probably unconsciously, I was starting to imitate my dad.

It only took two beers to make me mean. I'd fight anyone who crossed me, no matter how big. I'm not really a big person. I'm six feet tall, and I've always been thin. But when I got a few drinks in me, I lost control and became like a crazy person. I got into one scrape after another.

When I was in the tenth grade we were living in Rosenberg, Texas. Five guys in our neighborhood formed a band. Jerry knew them and talked to them from time to time. He'd even sit in on their jam sessions.

"We need a singer," one of them said. "We can play all right but we need someone to sing."

"My little brother can sing," Jerry said.

"Is he any good?"

"Good? He's great," Jerry answered. "He sings in church a lot."

"We don't need a church singer."

"Well, he's in the glee club at school."

One of them shrugged. "Tell him to come over and try out."

"You bet," Jerry said. "He's good. He sings like Ricky Nelson." Jerry hurried home and told me.

"Me? You kidding?"

"Hey, they need a singer and you sing good."

It had never occurred to me to audition. It made me mad that Jerry had volunteered for me to sing in public. It also scared me.

But it felt good to have Jerry as my best friend again. I went to the garage where they practiced. I had to compete with another singer. He imitated Elvis Presley's style. I just sang like me. They chose me.

We became known as The Triumphs. When I sang I hid behind the mike, afraid to let go. For the first ten years, I didn't move—I stood straight as a poker and hung on to that mike. I was always afraid I'd hit a sour note or foul up in some way. In those days I felt as if my whole manhood depended on singing every note perfectly.

Then we started getting bookings in little Texas towns. Most of the places looked like warehouses, but people came on weekends to drink and dance. I don't know how much of our music they heard. We were loud—especially in the beginning. And we began drinking and getting friendly with people. By the time a dance was over, we'd all be half-crocked and often ended up in a brawl.

We kept this up through high school and even after we managed to get to college. Somewhere near the end of my first semester I realized I had to make a change. Either I had to give myself to studying and making good grades, or I could play weekends and practice every night. I couldn't do both.

I dropped out of college thinking, *I can always go back,* but I didn't know if I would ever have another chance to get into music. Jerry dropped out of college too and became our manager. The others stayed in school, trying to keep up with both. For them music was relaxing—a hobby. For me, the only time I really felt alive was when I sang with the band. Then I could express myself and communicate with people. It was the only time in my life when I really felt worthwhile.

At our gigs, once in a while people would scream and stand up. I would sing my heart out for them.

Our group decided to try records. The Triumphs cut a total of eleven records. A few of them became local hits, because we got small-town disc jockeys to play them. The last couple played all over the Southwest.

In 1966 we recorded the Hank Williams song, "I'm So Lonesome I Could Cry." We were only one out of a hundred groups that recorded that song. But no one had ever made much of it except Hank Williams.

Surprisingly, our record got on the pop charts and became my first million-seller.

An old friend, Steve Tyrell, had gotten into the promotion business with Scepter Records. He had been working with Dionne Warwick. He told his bosses in New York about us.

It seems incredible now, but in those days we never saw what was happening. We were a group of naive Texas boys, enjoying our music and trying to make a little money. As each step came along we moved ahead, never thinking it unusual.

We began getting all kinds of offers after Steve helped us. Gene Pitney's Cavalcade of Stars offered us a chance to tour with them —along with fourteen or fifteen other acts. The band members didn't want to go.

"Too risky," one of them said.

Another had gone into a beer distributorship with his dad and felt he couldn't leave.

I went by myself and the tour people hired a new band, which they billed as The Triumphs. Glenn Spreen was the leader. The band played for me and for all of the other acts.

I became a solo on that tour. Eventually I recorded "Raindrops," which threw me into the international spotlight. Oddly enough Burt Bacharach and Hal David wrote that song for Bob Dylan and offered it to him first. Bob Dylan only sang his own music, so he turned it down. They came to me next. Ever since, the public has identified me with that song more than any others I've sung, and it has sold something like nine million copies.

Reflecting on my childhood, I realize it was lonely and filled with pain. I didn't think much of myself, and the important things like love, thoughtfulness, and kindness were denied me by my dad. But as my success increased, life never got any better at home, except that our roles had changed. Even though my success as a singer was minor, I became the head of the family. Dad was still alive, but everyone came to me. Mom even asked me about what to do with Judy when she came in late.

The family unconsciously made me the authority, because I was getting recognized locally as a singer. I was also making money. I felt often like a rich uncle the family didn't like. Just having the money somehow gave me a special position.

I had experimented with drugs since I first started with the band. For several years I had been sampling "pot." As my success grew,

I met others who used amphetamines and other drugs such as Quaaludes to get high. It was easy to get prescription drugs—an unlimited amount. And the longer I stayed in the music business, the more sources I discovered.

Then I was hooked. But I didn't know it for a long, long time.

21

On the Greens

People sometimes ask me, "B.J., what's your philosophy in life?"

That's not an easy question to answer. My philosophy has changed—especially since I turned to Jesus Christ in 1976.

My outlook began to change with a drastic transformation in January of that year. A miracle took place in my life. Not just my immediate release from drugs—and I don't want to minimize that —but I had one of those in-an-instant changes. Until then, all my experiences had taught and confirmed that life is hell and we aren't supposed to make it. At least not poor folks like me.

Instead of dealing with life, I learned to run from it. I learned from unspoken actions in our home to avoid complications and to shut out problems.

When I started making money early as a singer, it gave me a new view of life: Money can take the place of maturity. My ideas cost me millions of dollars to live out. Yet all the money I made never provided me with one night of restful sleep.

For instance, because of my need for Dad's love I unconsciously sought for my father everywhere. If an older man showed acceptance and sincerity toward me, I'd end up hiring him.

"We don't need a contract," I'd say, "your word is good enough."

Explosions came later when I'd discover that the "sincere" man had cheated me. Or when I'd realize he had a serious character flaw and I would totally reject him.

I didn't understand all that. I was thirty-three before I stopped looking for my father in other people. That's when I became a man who sincerely wanted to follow Jesus Christ.

As I grew in my Christian faith, I began to realize that life gives us choices. Life doesn't just dump on us like a random poker hand. But it took me a long time to understand that fact and much longer to change my behavioral patterns.

If the problems of a boy are too big to solve, then the problems of a man are beyond control. Without ever consciously putting those feelings into words, I functioned that way for years. I couldn't get the upper hand in life, so why try?

I made money in those early days—lots of it. I had gold records and all the fame that went with them. Yet I never felt successful. Not until my conversion to Jesus Christ and the events that followed my conversion did I feel successful as a human being. I am now emerging as a whole person. I am overcoming obstacles and growing in the kind of maturity that money can't get for me.

Immediately after my conversion, my career took second place. I wanted to know as much about Jesus Christ and the Christian message as I could. Gloria and I spent a lot of time together trying to sort life out.

The Christians we met in those early days helped us more than they'll ever know. They accepted us—without our having to prove anything. They taught us what the word *community* means. They helped us channel our energies and direct our talents.

I believe some of the songs I recorded during that period are among the best work of my career to that point. The Christian community provided loving care and constantly showed they were with us. They also provided protection for us until I could get it together. As I struggled to establish priorities—the importance of God, my own life, Gloria, and Paige—the believers protected us from the harsh realities of a cold world.

For the first six months we attended every worship service, Bible study, and seminar we could. We read books and watched dozens of TV preachers. Then we changed focus.

Gloria and I felt the need to spend more time together—getting to know each other and growing as a husband and wife. We also felt the need to absorb the information and apply what we'd heard.

That meant less time for seminars and Bible studies. We even began to stay away from the church that had brought us to Christ. We didn't leave because of a lack of love. We had to grow. We had to break away from them and learn to stand on our own in the same way a teen finally makes the break at home.

Gloria and I visited churches—usually those where I would not be recognized as "B.J. Thomas, singer." We wanted to relate to people as people and fellow believers.

Gloria put it this way, "We had a wonderful time in the 'emergency room church.' They met us in our time of crisis."

Although we no longer attend the Mid-Cities Bible Church, they were there when we needed them. They loved us when we couldn't even love ourselves.

And actually, that's always been the key problem in my life: lack of self-love, or as some call it, low self-esteem. My drug addiction only reinforced that concept. Just getting off the drugs didn't change me, but it made me free to find myself as a worthwhile person.

My relationship with Gloria went through rough stages. For most of our years together we had fought, screamed, or retreated into cold words or silence. These were the ways we had learned, as wounded children, to cope in life.

We found help from many places in making these changes.

Perhaps the best way to write about my struggles and growth is to mention the significant steps.

First, a group of Christians surrounded us and, most of all, loved us and taught us about the love of God expressed through people.

Second, counseling sessions helped. Gloria has already written about several of our experiences—and most of them let us down in one way or another. But we always got enough benefit from them so that we kept going back or changing to another counselor.

We learned that, with our varied backgrounds and with what Gloria calls our dysfunctional living skills, it takes a long time to change, even under professional and trained guidance. We learned, for instance, to save up our hostilities and confusion for those sessions. Instead of blowing up over all kinds of things each day, we learned to save up and explode in a counselor's office—in safe territory.

We made it a rule that when we were having fun and family times, we would not let our problems intrude. We didn't always keep to that rule, as Gloria has pointed out, but we knew it was a rule. When we exploded at an inappropriate time, we knew we had to be doubly careful the next time.

The first thing we learned in counseling is that we had focused on symptoms and not on causes. I yelled a lot at Gloria for years, then I worked at controlling my temper instead of asking *why* I yelled.

We learned to get to the basic causes. That took time, and it proved painful to change thirty-three years of behavioral patterns.

Third, we grappled with the business last. One bad experience led to another because we kept hiring the wrong people. I finally turned over the business end to Gloria. That may sound like a simple statement. It came about after much struggle. I knew Gloria had the ability—she's a marvelously capable woman. I also knew that someone with my interests at heart had to handle those affairs.

The difficulty for me lay in giving her that position. Having come from the macho-type background, I had never known a woman to function as a partner, or as the Bible says, "a help, fit for him."

I learned to accept her opinions. I marveled at how she grasped the details of our business and set us up on a sound footing. My wife could do what a dozen managers, agents, and lawyers had not accomplished in nearly twenty years!

We're now a team. We don't struggle with manipulating each other. Decisions come easier. Our relationship to each other has continued to improve. As a result, we're both better Christians, and we're still growing.

Fourth, drugs controlled my life for years, then they disappeared. A healthy person finds a replacement. I found mine in golf. On the greens I found a healthy way to funnel my obsession and to really get inside myself.

Some find their release through jogging or swimming. I found mine with a 4-iron in my hand.

After being on the road for two weeks, singing before thousands, talking to hundreds of people, giving interviews, and rushing from place to place, I need a place of retreat. Walking down the landscaped fairways provides that retreat.

Golf calls for such total concentration that I have to clear my head of all pressures. On a subconscious level, I began to notice beautiful trees sprinkled over the course. Bushes flowered. Even birds occasionally flew overhead.

At first, I spent enough time in the rough to be a caretaker. I could hit my ball within twenty feet of a resident squirrel, with no concern from the squirrel. He had probably watched me play enough to know that my ball posed no threat.

The time I spent on the greens was so peaceful, and after a while I realized I had a natural talent for the game. I began setting goals for improving my golf. I got the club pro to give me pointers.

As he helped me, I achieved better scores and improved form. I also discovered some of the frustrations of golf. Some days I would shoot in the seventies and the next day I would go back and play in the high nineties.

One day I saw that golf paralleled my life. On those greens I discovered how to apply the principles I had been learning. Golf requires skill and mental concentration. I spent enough time on the practice tee to develop the skill, resulting in a decent golf swing.

As far as mental concentration goes, I saw another parallel. All kinds of things restricted my relationships with people. As I concentrated on discovering why I behaved as I did, I also received help in changing. Then my relationships improved. In the same way, I learned to shut out noises and problems as I faced the tee. Then my game improved.

For example, when I first became a Christian, I realized that if I wanted to understand the Christian life, I had to study the Bible and spend time and energy in knowing God. The same with the golf swing. I had to learn good techniques before I could expect to hit the ball well every time.

Even after learning good form, I had to hit the ball enough times to ingrain a good swing into "muscle memory." I saw that clearly.

For a long time, I didn't see the parallel quite as clearly in dealing with some of my problems. The experience with my golf swing brought home the idea to me of how handicapped I was without techniques for making good decisions.

When I came to the golf course, I brought a lot of anxieties with me. I would start out tense. But because I took such a keen interest in the sport, I did everything I knew to make myself a better player. But my golf game (at first) became just another kind of life situation. I applied incorrect techniques. I remained tense. One by one I had to relearn the proper ways to play a good game.

When I started exploring my anxious feelings concerning my golf game in the counseling sessions, my game improved. Then, when I saw how to go about making myself a better player, I began applying those same principles to dealing with other areas of my life.

That may sound easy, but it wasn't. The boy's problems were finally getting answers, so that the life of the man could develop. I spent so much time struggling over my golf game, sometimes I'm surprised that I stayed with it.

I'm glad I stayed with the game. I spend time on the greens not only enjoying the game, but also enjoying just being with the Lord. I talk to Him and feel His presence.

I learn more about myself and understand myself as I play a game I love.

At times golf gets in the way of something I ought to do or an errand Gloria wants me to run. On most mornings when I'm home, I have her blessings when I leave. She understands the positive effect that golf has on me.

22

Good-bye Macho Man

Here's a husband's view on marriage.

When Gloria and I were married in December 1968, we entered into a traditional southern marriage. I was the man, the head of the household. That meant I provided and protected. Gloria was the woman, the wife whom I took care of; and she stayed home, mothered children, and scrubbed floors.

We lived by our ingrained understanding that a woman only needed a man to take care of her, and he expected her to meet his emotional and sexual needs.

Underneath those well-defined roles, I, like many other southern husbands, expected Gloria to make life happy for me. She was somehow supposed to provide peace of mind because I brought in money. We depended on each other to supply our needs, but we didn't really know what our needs were.

We never put those concepts into words. Maybe if we had, we could have dealt with them earlier. We both lived on assumptions. After all, I had no other pattern in life. It never occurred to me to be different.

So, when life did not measure up or I was unhappy, like my father before me, I blamed my wife. Of course it's irrational, but I didn't see that.

Both of us had such low self-esteem. We really didn't know how to fully love each other because we didn't know how to be loved. We couldn't really take care of our individual selves, much less give strength to each other.

Here's how I see dysfunctional living skills in operation:

Husband Jim comes home from work. Wife Helen is talking on the phone. "Honey, get me a clean shirt."

She says, "I've got to hang up now because Jim needs a shirt."

He interrupted her conversation. To him, his immediate need for a shirt was more important than her finishing a conversation with a friend.

Suppose Jim did this to Helen on a regular basis? The message eventually becomes, "What I want is more important than what you want."

I know that when I'd pull this kind of stunt, Gloria said she would feel a tightness in her throat and chest. She'd sink into depression. I made her feel as though she should have anticipated my need and that she had failed because I had to ask.

Gloria began accepting the idea that what she was doing either wasn't important or at least was not equal to my activity. Yet, even as she slowly accepted that concept as true, it only made her feel more insecure and useless.

Gloria and I had problems more serious than my interrupting her on the phone. Ours had become (although not in words) a lord-to-slave relationship.

When I found myself involved in a problem or project and it got uncomfortable for me to deal with, I'd follow the pattern I had learned in childhood and dump it on Gloria. After all, I was the man. I was supposed to handle things—I did, by dumping them on her.

The more I played Macho Man, the more I suppressed Gloria's talents and creativity. And the greater the conflict. I could not understand why she wanted to fight all the time. I knew the rules. And I went by my rules.

I learned, after years of conflict, we both went by rules. But it was as though I played by the rules of football and she was following basketball rules. Neither of us quite understood why the other wouldn't cooperate.

This sounds a little simpler than it really was, of course, but it showed up in hundreds of ways. For instance, Gloria, a beautiful and talented person, never felt she was my equal. Gloria writes beautiful music, but never took time to develop her skill. She does now. She always felt (and it took me years to learn) that I disapproved of the way she dressed or wore her hair. Actually, I was always proud of Gloria in public. I just didn't realize she needed to know that.

Gloria assumed she had no opinion worth offering. Or that even when she felt she was right her words fell on deaf ears. I demanded submission. She either gave in and resented it or she fought back. She never really had a choice.

I demanded submission—after all, many of our Christian friends showed that the Bible demands women to submit. I've learned that true submission comes from the heart. True Christians submit *to each other*—as the next natural thing.

Submission becomes a problem when both people are not complete in themselves. When both try to please each other, the matter of submission really isn't an issue.

I once asked Robert Schuller about this. He said, "If Arvella ever submitted, she wouldn't be the woman I married." And I've been around the Schullers enough to realize what a great marriage and deep relationship those two share.

Gloria and I wanted the same kind of relationship that we've observed with people like the Schullers and Billy and Ruth Graham. It took us a long time before we got to that point.

Several times Gloria asked me, "If we love each other, why do we spend so much time misunderstanding each other?"

We finally learned that getting the relationship right would take time. It would be a process—a process of learning and maturing. It would also require commitment.

For months we searched through our backgrounds, thinking and reexamining. We asked, "Why did I behave this way?" or "What made me say that?"

Both of us also realized that our backgrounds programmed us to fail. When we had success we didn't know what to do with it or about it. When I had succeeded as a singer, I counteracted by failing as a husband and as a parent. My health deteriorated.

I realize so much of it goes back to the way my dad conditioned me. "Some of us aren't supposed to make it in this life, Billy."

I realize in looking back that when I didn't win the Grammy Award for "Raindrops" I felt relief inside. I yelled and threw things in my dressing room, but it was all an act. I didn't win because I wasn't *supposed* to win at anything.

I no longer feel that way. Through Jesus Christ I have gained resources I didn't have before. Besides that, Gloria and I have developed a system of dealing with conflicts.

Having a difference between us no longer signals the end of our worlds. If I treat her unfairly, she no longer has to accept that kind of treatment.

She has learned to make her decisions on her own. I have learned to make mine. We make choices out of sincere love for each other, but we are both individuals and cannot depend on the other to choose for us.

This matter of making our own decisions has given us greater respect for each other. We handle conflict better now. I've learned to listen to Gloria. She's got a better business head than I do. When we come to a conflict in business matters, I've learned to listen carefully to what she says. She's usually right.

We can do that now because neither of us is a threat to the other. We love each other more than ever. But we also respect each other *as people,* as well as mates.

I've learned a lot since my conversion to Jesus Christ. I see now, as I didn't before, that everything we do makes an imprint on our physical and emotional makeup. We are the end result of every moment that we have lived. We decide much of today's actions because of how we decided in the past—or how we were taught in the past.

We're both learning that we don't have to continue the way we used to be. We are still becoming new people. With God's help and with our love, we're getting better all the time.

It's not easy to write about the problems Gloria and I went through. Yet both of us feel it's important to share what goes on behind the scenes.

We've come a long way. We're more sensitive to each other than ever before. We were both absolutely discordant for so many years. And now that we've learned to "make beautiful music together," we're finding out how good life can really be!

The Singer

It's a life mixed in singles and albums of gold
And platinum platters when great songs are told,
A life of hotel rooms and room service tips,
And then smaller motel rooms when fame starts to slip.

It's a life filled with worry that the magic won't last,
And mirrors reflect that some more years have passed.
And doubts begin creeping inside of your brain,
Singing lyrics no fresher than last summer's rain.

So—you hum in your car,
Tap your pillow at night
In hopes, by some miracle,
Words come out right.
For singers with wrong words
Don't last very long.
So—won't somebody write me a half-decent song?

KYLE ROTE

23

Gloria Jean

Now that B.J. has written about his background and childhood, I want to write about mine.

As I think about my growing-up years, I remember the words of a psychologist we went to. "Gloria," he said, "80 percent of a child's emotional development occurs within the first six years of life."

If that's true (and I don't doubt it), I realize now why I had so many struggles to become what another psychologist calls a fulfilled self.

My mother named me after a pretty teen singing star of the Hollywood B films—Gloria Jean. She had dark hair, large blue eyes, and a beautiful singing voice. Maybe my mother hoped I'd be like Gloria Jean, I don't know.

I was born October 15, 1949, in Lynchburg, Virginia, the second of four children.

My father, Harold Richardson, worked in air conditioning and heating most of the time. But he had tried all kinds of blue-collar jobs over the years. In my childhood, our standard of living fluctuated between moderately poor, poor, and flat broke. Most of the time we were only moderately poor.

My father dominated our house with a heavy hand. He often said, "Anybody under my roof has to do what I say." We knew he meant it.

The actual doing of what he wanted was rarely pleasant. A battered child himself, he told of his experiences of being brutalized and neglected. His own deprived childhood resulted in bottled-up frustration and anger.

My father was a combination of contradictions: exciting, compassionate, and pleasant, but also brutal, harsh, and intolerant.

We had two general moods in our house—when Dad was home and when he was gone. When he was home we had to remain quiet. Even so he constantly barked, "Will you kids shut up in there?"

Sometimes he'd just walk up and slap us without warning. Often we had no idea what made him angry, and we seldom asked. The question only brought a heavier slap.

My mother, Louise Marie Campbell, a moody woman, fluctuated from temper outbursts to an outlandish, clowning humor.

Her sharp wit could cut anyone down. She had a frankness about her that I inherited. She often said openly, "I only married your dad to get away from home."

"But didn't you love him?" I asked once.

"I was too stupid to know better, so I thought I loved him."

In her better moods, Mom loved parties. At home, she would often turn on soul music and dance to it, or laugh and sing popular songs.

She, too, had come from a home where her father beat her and made life unbearable.

For sixteen years my parents' marriage survived. We moved regularly. I'm not sure how many schools I attended. The number could be as high as twenty. Every time I try to count it up, I reach a different total. One thing moving around taught me to do was to adjust quickly to people. It also taught me to survive.

In my early years, I felt close to my mother. She confided in me and talked to me constantly. I felt loved, and I believed we had a very special relationship.

As I grew older Harry, my older brother, and I became closer. We often felt that we had each other and no one else. It was as though we said, "Together we can survive in this world."

My childhood memories are blurred. A procession of houses, in different towns, in different states—and our never staying long enough to really belong. We were always afraid to get too close to people, because we knew Dad would make us move on soon.

I wanted close friends. And it seemed that every time I'd establish a friendship with someone, Dad would come home and say, "Well, time to pack up."

"We're not moving again!" Mother would scream.

Once in a while, we raised our voices, too.

"But I keep doing bad in school because we move around so much," Harry said.

"No wonder we stay broke," Mom argued. "We move, stay a few months or a year, and then we're off again. Never get a chance to save or to settle in or—"

"I am the man of this house!" he would interrupt. "What I say goes. And I say we move!"

Mother argued and screamed until Dad said those words. When he made a statement like that, she knew she couldn't fight anymore.

Basically Dad was a dreamer, always looking for the big opportunity in the next town. He always expected to better himself with our next move. He dreamed and he promised, but he never produced.

When I'd remind him, "Dad, you promised a nice house for us. Look at this dump—" he'd slap my face or knock me down. Physical reaction was the only way he knew how to respond. He could never admit mistakes.

This incident with Spot may help give an idea of our life.

We lived in Knoxville, Tennessee, in the country. Harry had already started to school, and we acquired a dog we called Spot. He was a shaggy-haired, medium-sized mutt of questionable origin, with spots on his body and around one eye.

Harry and I became attached to Spot and spent every minute we could with him, playing with him, feeding him, trying to teach him tricks. He was the most welcome relief we had from an oppressive childhood.

One day Dad said, "We're going to get rid of that mutt."

"Get rid of him? We can't!" I yelled back.

"He's too much trouble. Always wanting in and out of the house. Barking. Always in the way. . . ."

"Please Dad, we'll keep him quiet and—"

"I said we're getting rid of Spot!"

The next day he took the dog, put him in the car, and drove across town. As he later told us, he stopped, let Spot out, and drove away.

Mother didn't care much for animals, but that day she stood with her arms around us and cried when Dad pulled out of the driveway with Spot. Harry stood silently for a moment and then, as the car disappeared from sight, he screamed, "I hate you! I hate you for stealing our dog!"

When Dad got home, I said, "Why couldn't we keep Spot?"

"Because I say we can't! And if you don't like it, little lady, I'll slap you in the mouth."

Several days later, Mother opened the front door. Spot jumped up and barked. He was filthy, skinny, and smelled terrible, but it was our Spot. When he saw me, he ran up to me, his mud-covered paws went around me, and he licked my face. Within minutes we were both filthy, but I didn't care. Spot was back. It made everything wonderful.

After Spot's return, we just knew it would all work out. Dad couldn't send our dog away again.

When Dad came home we ran to him and, all blabbing at once, told him the story.

"And please, you will let us keep him, won't you?"

Even Mother, in a soft voice, begged him.

Dad listened and didn't say anything for a long time. Finally letting out a string of swear words, he said, "We're sure not taking him when we move from here."

"Just for now," I pleaded, satisfied that we had won a reprieve for Spot.

"I'm not going to start lugging some mutt all over the place." He said a lot more words, mostly swearing and complaining. We didn't pay much attention. Spot was home. He was ours!

It wasn't long, however, before the dreaded announcement came: "We're moving to Georgia."

That simple. Dad made the rules and then decided when to enforce them.

"Can Spot go with us?"

"Nope. We're not going to live in the country," he said. "It's a housing project—a nice place in the city. Lots of people and kids. Good schools. But they don't allow dogs."

I don't remember our answer, only that Harry and I tried to figure out how to keep the dog. We tried pleading to no avail. We also had the idea that if we begged long enough he might give in. We didn't worry about the bruises and the curses. We wanted Spot!

Mother finally said, "It's not the dog. It's the way you keep tormenting those kids. Let them have Spot."

"I'll decide if we keep that dog or not. So stop trying to tell me what to do!"

Harry and I tried everything we could think of. We ran away one day but Dad found us. We tried to hide Spot in a large box, but Dad saw what we were planning. Dad spanked us after each attempt and lectured us.

Until the day before we moved, we begged and pleaded. By then we all faced reality: Dad wouldn't give in. I realize now that we had pushed him too far. He didn't know how to back down, and he wasn't going to do it this time either.

We finally arranged with neighbors to take care of our dog. They understood our dad. They, along with us, kept hoping Dad would change his mind.

Daddy and a man he worked with loaded a borrowed truck and started packing. Mother, Harry, and I stood by the truck, pleading for him to let us keep Spot.

Daddy didn't say much—he was too busy carrying out furniture and boxes.

"Get in," he said when he had tied up everything.

"But, Daddy—" I made one last attempt.

His eyes met mine. "I said, *get in!*"

Mother and the two younger ones, Joyce and Tracy, got inside the cab of the pickup with him. The man helped Harry and me find a place in the back of the canvas-covered truck.

"Daddy, please," Harry cried out. "He won't be any trouble!"

"Shut up, you dumb kids back there!" He took a swat at Harry and missed.

I knew the final answer.

Peeping over the tailgate, we saw Spot, wagging his tail and barking. Dad got in front and started the engine. As he drove off, Spot started running after us.

At first he kept up with us, and Harry and I screamed and cried, "Keep coming, Spot!"

I had never experienced such pain as I watched Spot, panting and trying to run as fast as the truck. His chest swelled, caved in, we could see he was dropping back. As the truck left the dirt road and turned onto the two-lane highway, we saw Spot dropping back.

Then the truck stopped for a traffic light, and the dog appeared again, trying for all he was worth to catch us.

This agonizing chase went on for miles.

"You'll kill that poor dog, egging him on like that." Finally the man sitting in the back of the truck with us put the tarp down, so we couldn't see anymore.

"Go back! Go back, Spot!" I screamed through my tears. He was already so far away from home.

The man started crying, too. He picked up both Harry and me, put us on his lap, and hugged us tight. We all sat quite still, tears falling down our cheeks.

"I hate him. I'll always hate him!" Harry said, teeth clinched. I knew who he meant.

I finally fell asleep, dreaming that Spot had caught up and was now resting in my arms.

Just before dark, we pulled into the housing project. The pickup hadn't even come to a stop when Harry and I stared at each other. Tears filled my eyes. *We saw at least six dogs running around the area.*

Before I was eight years old, I had two experiences with males that affected my life positively.

First my brother Harry, three years older than I, did a lot for me. We played together constantly—he the leader and I the follower. Harry had such a vivid imagination, and we often played pirates and fought with homemade swords.

More than the games, Harry took care of me when we were small.

He constantly encouraged me by saying things like, "I'm proud of you" or "You're great." Even now, although I'm an adult and no longer in contact with my brother, I realize how much I miss him and how greatly he influenced the first eight years of my life when we were the closest. My dad used to say that because of Harry I had a fairy-tale outlook on life. Maybe I did—at least, because of his encouragement, I knew things could be better. He encouraged me to keep looking for the brighter side.

The second experience was with my dad in what I call our one sensitive exchange in life. It only lasted a few hours, but I've never forgotten. It showed me a side of him that I had never seen before.

When I was four, my mother became pregnant. Of course, I was too young to realize what was going on. One day when she was gone, Dad came home from work.

"Come on, Gloria," he said, "let's go for a ride."

I could hardly believe it. Harry was in school, and Dad came home just for me—to do something *with me*. We got into Dad's big, old, black car. "Where do you want to go?" he asked.

Surprised, I said I'd like to drive by Harry's school. We did that, I mentioned several other places and he took me.

Dad had never treated me that way before. I'd always been afraid of him and that look on his face said, "If you mess with me, you're asking for trouble." But on that day his face relaxed.

He acted as though he enjoyed being with me. He teased me and I laughed. There was such a difference between then and the way we always had to please him. That day he seemed to concentrate on making me happy. And I knew he loved me—not just because he was good to me, but a deeper and different side of my father emerged—a tender, caring side.

Finally we stopped at a store. He bought me a toy and ice cream. He took my hand, and we walked through the store together. He stopped and talked to people, telling them about his pretty little girl. I knew he felt proud of me.

Later he pulled up at a gas station. Dad bought me a Coke and sat me on the hood of the car while he went inside to use the phone. A minute later he came back. "Get down now, Gloria."

I started climbing down and said, "Daddy, can I have some potato chips?"

"No," he snapped back. "Just get in the car."

I scrambled down, jumped inside, and sat in the backseat.

"Best surprise for today, Gloria," he said, "is waiting back at the house."

As he said those words I looked at his face in the rearview mirror; it had changed—he was becoming the old dad again. The wonderful father I had spent time with and who had loved me was gone again.

We arrived home. It surprised me to discover Mama was back. I ran to her room and threw open the door. She lay in bed and beside her was a red, screaming baby.

"This is your baby sister, Joyce. Do you want us to keep her, Gloria?"

I looked at that screaming baby, blue veins sticking out and bald head. "No. Send her back." I foolishly believed we could do that.

For a long time I used to think about that day with my dad. It had been wonderful. He loved me—and I knew it. Some girls have those kinds of experiences all their lives. I had it only once—but that single experience stayed with me the rest of my life.

I often sat and let my mind relive that magical day. I thought that my dad was like a noble prince, and that he loved me. My magic day ended, but I've never forgotten it.

24

Love at First Sight

I started school in Georgia. But there would be many houses and many schools to follow. Only snatches of events from the next few years remain in my memory. I would hardly get to know classmates before we moved again. The lack of permanence in my life still causes me to have difficulty remembering names and addresses.

Still, despite the moves, we held together as a family.

In spite of everything, I loved Dad. He scared me and I never knew his moods, but I loved him. He was a man with many problems and pressures—a man who didn't know how to cope with life. He did most of his problem solving by running away or fighting with his fists.

That's the only family life I knew.

We moved to Gastonia, North Carolina, just before I entered fourth grade. We lived there three and a half years—the longest in any one place.

That's also where the family disintegrated. My mother started to work, and she and my dad both worked hard, saved money, and bought a country store. After that both of them started to drink heavily, and Dad also gambled. At one party, my dad gambled away everything and lost the store.

My parents fought more, and Mother often left, staying away for weeks at a time. We would wake up and see blood on the walls and floor. At first it scared us, but after a while we accepted it as evidence that they had had one of their fights again. Over the years they had changed from being close and fun-loving to being distant and finally openly hostile.

During that time Mother turned on me and screamed at me constantly. I seemed never to do anything that pleased her. She would walk up to me and scratch my arms or slap my face. Sometimes she forced me to sit for hours while she called the other children in.

"See how I reward good boys and girls," and she handed each of them a dime. "If Gloria knew how to be a good girl, she could have a dime, too."

I started to cry, not knowing what I had done wrong.

"It's too late for tears, Gloria," she said. "Next time, if you're good like the others, you'll have a dime, too."

"Please, Mama, I didn't do anything—"

"I hate you! You stupid, hateful girl. You make life miserable for me and for everyone around here."

After lengthy abuse from her I finally said, "I hate you, too!"

She struck me across the face, and my mouth started bleeding. "I still hate you no matter what you do to me!"

She struck me again.

"I wish you'd leave this time and never come back!" I determined to have the last word, even if it turned out to be my last word in life.

I didn't have to wait long for her to leave. Within a few days she had walked out again. Daddy took off someplace, too. Neither of them said anything, they just left. The four of us stayed alone in the house for three days. Then, in the middle of the third night, Daddy came into the house, got the four of us, and told us to grab whatever clothes we could. He threw the hurriedly packed boxes into the trunk and backseat. Within thirty minutes we were gone.

For the next two years our lives and future were completely uncertain. We never knew who we would be living with. Mom would take us away from Dad, and then he'd take us back again.

In many ways it didn't matter whom we lived with. The fights continued, although they were a little more physical with Daddy and more of the screaming–slapping type with Mama.

More than once Dad said to me, "You shut your smart mouth or I'll put you in an orphanage!"

For a long time that had frightened me. As I grew older it began to appeal to me. At least then I could stay in one place. One day I yelled back, "Fine! Put me there!"

"I will!"

By the time I reached fourteen, I decided he wouldn't threaten me again. "You just do that. I'll have you up on charges!"

"You just shut your mouth, or I'll stick you in an orphanage for sure!"

"I'll have you locked up for being an unfit parent. They'll make it tough on you for your drinking and slapping us all the time. You just go ahead!"

"You think you're so smart," he said.

But Daddy never again threatened to send me to an orphanage.

Mother and Daddy fought from state to state. I don't think either of them really wanted us. It was just that they had learned to hate each other so much, that neither of them wanted the other to have us. That left us in the middle. It was a painful life.

In my early teens, I was lonely and afraid. I remember having clammy hands much of the time. I would lie awake, wondering if I would ever be happy. Wishing that someone, someday would love me. Then I'd think, *I'm not any good and not worth loving.*

Oddly enough, as I grew older, Dad and I grew closer. We were both disoriented and lonely. We held on to each other, the way a drowning person clutches a piece of driftwood. When my parents' game of spite-and-run finally stopped, Dad had custody of us four kids. It was like Russian roulette with four kids in the loaded chamber. I don't think Daddy intended or wanted to end up with us. He just used the tactic to control my mother.

I was ten when Mother left for good, and for six years we didn't see her again. During those six years we moved from one rented trailer to another. We did the best we could to survive.

We sold illegal, homemade, insect pads, supposed to keep away mosquitos—they didn't. Dad made me walk into poor, black neighborhoods to sell them. While still underage, I tried cooking in greasy, roadside diners. We did anything we could to bring in money.

And I survived.

Dad finally dropped the pretense of being concerned about our welfare. He often disappeared for four days at a time. On more than one occasion, we actually stole to have enough food to eat. Harry ran away at thirteen, coming back periodically and then, after heated arguments with Dad, taking off again.

I realized that I, too, was on my own. No one would take care of Gloria Richardson. If she was to survive, she'd have to do it on her own. Finally understanding my situation gave me the ability to make decisions. It forced me to grow up too soon and to live on an adult level.

Dad usually lived with us—along with a series of "stepmothers." Dad never married any of them. In fact, even after my parents' separation, it took eleven years before they finally divorced.

I graduated from high school at seventeen—the only one in my family ever to do so. I did well in school. Despite the moving around constantly, I maintained an average between B and C. Although I may have had an average IQ, I made up for anything I lacked with determination. That determination kept me going. My teen years developed in me a cold-steel will to survive.

I left home almost immediately after graduation. I had only what I wore and a few things in a brown paper bag. I would make it on my own. And I did.

I modeled in local stores, wrote for local Houston publications, and worked as a salesgirl.

I knew that as long as I could control my life I would make it. Deep inside me, however, lurked one fear. Somehow, something would happen and I wouldn't be able to stay in control.

Then, on September 17, 1967, my whole life changed.

I answered the phone. It was William. We didn't know each other well but found we could talk to each other, like a brother-and-sister relationship.

"How about going out with me for a drive?"

"Will, I'm tired—I really am—"

"Gloria, I just need a friend tonight. Someone to talk to."

I couldn't refuse that. He picked me up at the apartment I shared with another girl. We drove for a while, and then he pulled onto the expressway. I knew he had been drinking, although I didn't think he had had much. He accelerated, changing lanes, passing every car. We pulled into the right lane, and suddenly a parked car appeared in the darkness ahead of us. Will tried to pull into the left lane, but he never made it. He slammed into the back of the parked car, spinning us around, and knocking us back into the car a second time.

I remember only that my face went through the windshield at least twice. A wave of numbness hit me, and I felt no pain. I couldn't move or talk. For a moment I even wondered if I was dead.

I heard voices talking and police sirens and I lay crumpled somewhere between the front seat and the floor. I could hear but couldn't respond to anything going on around me. I do remember being lifted out of the car and placed on some kind of stretcher.

The ambulance carried me to Houston's Memorial Hospital. I lost two teeth—knocked out in the impact—had a cracked jawbone, and a broken kneecap. Worst of all, it took four hundred stitches to sew up my face.

The injury to my face gave me the most concern. I've always been attractive. While I'm not tall enough (I'm only five feet five) for high-fashion modeling, I did well modeling in local stores and in Houston newspaper ads. My success and my income depended on my appearance. Even more, it was my only key to independence.

I spent three weeks in the hospital. As I recuperated, I forced myself to assess my situation. Through tears of pain and despair, I kept saying, "I'm going to make it. I'm going to make it."

I had survived seventeen years of life. I wouldn't give in now.

In assessing the situation I realized it would be a long time before I could hold down a regular job. I worried a lot. I was scared all the time. *But I've gotten through so many tough times in my life,* I would remind myself.

While in the hospital I wrote every family member I could think of. "I've been badly hurt in an automobile wreck. I have no money and no place to go. Can you help me? Can you send me anything?"

No one even answered.

During my entire recuperation period after leaving Memorial Hospital, I took only one bottle of aspirin for pain. Not because I didn't need more. I simply didn't have the money to have my prescriptions filled or even buy more aspirin.

I went home to live with Dad. It was an unbearable situation, and getting out of that house became the prime thought on my mind. I was scared all the time, not of him, but of how I would cope. For such a long time I couldn't even walk. My first steps after the accident were back out of my daddy's front door.

His lack of compassion coming after the lack of responses to my letters really confirmed that I was on my own. No one else would take care of me.

A girl friend let me stay in her apartment. At first I just cleaned and cooked. Then I fixed other girls' hair and they paid me. I wrote fillers for *Key* magazine in Houston. I made tables out of throwaway barrels. Anything I could think of that would bring in a dollar, I did.

I fixed up our apartment so creatively that other girls paid me to decorate theirs.

When I could finally get out and work, long after the scars had healed, I started in sales in the junior department of Houston's Smart Shop. Within nine months I had worked in every department and done everything from assisting the cosmetician to dressing manikins. Eventually I ran the junior department and helped make decisions on what items to buy. When I quit it gave my ego a great boost to learn that they hired *three* people to replace me!

I avoided the luxury of falling in love like the other girls. I had a single focus: survival.

I wasn't looking for a man to help me survive. I had only known one man—my father—and he provided no role model to enchant me.

Then, a month after my eighteenth birthday, the most remarkable thing happened. I went with two girl friends to Van's Ballroom in Houston.

I saw a man. Tall, skinny, with curly, brown hair and bluish green eyes. He appeared to me to be a knight in shining armor. For the

first time in my life, the dream man I had always imagined had a face.
When B.J. and I met, it was love at first sight.

Gloria

Despite your youth, we sense in you
A more matured and calmer view
Than that which has consumed your life
As confidante and loving wife

With talents of your own to tend
You seem to choose, instead to bend
An exit from the center stage
Remarkable!—for one your age

And, as new friends, it is our choice
To love a "heart" as much as "voice"
And pleases us that "voice" had heart
Enough to fashion his fresh start.

We also sense that you're his rock
To shield him from a thoughtless "knock"
And, in the end, when raindrops fall—
Because of you—you both stand tall.

KYLE ROTE

25

Empty Promises

B.J. and I had come a long way together since his conversion in 1976. That's when we both began getting our lives together with God and with each other. We'd also begun to experience how good life can be when two people love each other and work toward a better marriage.

Finally, in 1980, we started getting our business in tune also. We had long been aware of the need, but our personal lives took priority.

In August of 1980, for instance, it looked as though we had everything fairly well set up. Working with a woman who fronted for us, I signed a contract for a book with the Fleming H. Revell Publishing Company. We planned for her to administrate the business while I spent the major portion of my time on the book.

The setup looked great. I would write, check occasionally on the business, and spend the rest of my time raising two infants and my almost baby-sitting-aged daughter. Unfortunately, the woman and I both realized that the relationship would not work, and we parted.

I found myself left to write the book, administrate the business, *and* try to raise a family.

The work load overwhelmed me. *Lord, how can I possibly get it all done?*

I agonized for days, trying to do the best I could. Even after fourteen-hour work days, I felt as though I had scarcely accomplished anything.

Then a sudden ray of hope appeared. It happened this way.

B.J. and I had been continuing our sessions with a Christian counselor for a year. He had helped us more than any of the others we had gone to.

One day he called. "Could you and B.J. meet me for lunch? I have a proposal you might be interested in."

We met him the next day at a restaurant. Immediately after we ordered, he said, "You two have done well in our sessions together."

He paused and smiled, obviously making sure we understood. "In fact, I don't think you need me anymore."

"Really?" I asked as I squeezed B.J.'s hands.

He nodded. "You two have come a long, long way. You've overcome unrealistic expectations in life. You've learned to accept and deal realistically with each other."

B.J. didn't say much, but his face showed me that he was as pleased as I was.

"So now," he said, "you two need to just live for a while. I'm always available if you run into an impasse. But you've learned so much. I think you can handle almost anything." For several minutes he reviewed the space we had covered.

Yes, I thought, *we have come a long way together. A long way.*

"Now," he said, "I asked you to lunch to celebrate that occasion. I also have another reason."

"Sure, what's that?" B.J. asked.

"I'm concerned about your business," he said. "In session after session you've talked about the way people have used you. You need help and you need it from someone who can set your systems straight."

"We need that all right," I agreed.

"What you need," he said, "is a person to come in, like a consultant, and get your business on a sound basis. Then, once you have it all set up, you can hire almost anybody, monitor them, but the business will almost run itself and run itself successfully."

He paused and then said, "Here's my proposal: I'd like to set up a system for you. I've done this before, you know."

Neither B.J. nor I knew anything of his background and previous experience. We knew only that he was a psychologist, had been recommended by a friend, and had helped us in our personal growth.

"Oh, yes," he said. "One company I worked for, with fifty employees, had everything going for it except sound business procedures. Within a few months I had them set up and they moved ahead. They're prospering today."

I became excited. I never doubted his ability. B.J., however, was slightly skeptical, although he said nothing to indicate it.

Both B.J. and I knew we needed help. B.J. couldn't possibly get involved in the business end while maintaining a full-time career on the road. He came home not to absorb himself in intricate business deals, but to rest and retreat before getting ready to go out again.

"You don't need to reinvent the wheel every time a new offer comes in. With standard forms, step-by-step procedures, and categorized operational objectives, you can take the heavy pressures off yourselves."

B.J. and I talked it over. Despite B.J.'s questions and hesitancies, we hired our former counselor as a business associate.

Show business, like any specialized field, has its own set of rules. You have to know your way around in order to function. We didn't have time to keep hiring new people to come in cold and make hundreds of mistakes while learning the rules.

But by coming in like an efficiency expert that giant companies hire, he could set up a system and help us put it into effect. I envisioned his developing into a valuable partner.

"You see," he said, "you have problems with the people you hire because they start out in business relationships. Then they soon find themselves involved in your personal lives. They lose perspective and objectivity."

"That makes sense," I said.

"I want to help correct all that," he said.

Everything he said made sense, so we hired him. B.J. and I had been trying to work together taking care of the business, and now I could concentrate on completing the book I had contracted for.

I waited for our new counselor to put the efficient system into practice. After two months I asked him about it.

"It takes time, you know," he said, a smile on his face. "First I need to understand all the complexities of the business. I need to know everything. Then I can assess all the weaknesses to prevent problems before they occur."

"It just seems like it's taking a long time," I said.

"I'm working very hard on it, Gloria. The music business is complex. I still need more information, but we'll have the system in operation soon."

I waited another three weeks. Not being the most patient person around, I asked point-blank, "When?"

We got into a discussion that took almost an hour. At the end of that time he still had never actually answered the question, I realize now, but he soothed me.

Four weeks later he sat down with B.J. and me, and we wrote our statement of philosophy.

"We plan to move into MBO—" he paused, "Management by Objective—and once we have envisioned exactly what we want accomplished, then we can make it easier to accomplish."

I felt more hope that day than I had since we had first hired him. At last we were getting something done. We started putting it down on paper and even drew an organizational chart. "That way, every person in the chain of command will know his or her responsibilities. No one can blame anyone else," our ex-counselor said.

Our philosophy statement covered everything from song writing to publishing to concerts. We wanted a method to handle songs sent to us by professionals and nonprofessionals. We get approximately a thousand letters a month. We schedule personal appearances and speaking engagements and plan how to merchandize albums, tapes, and books.

After another two months, nothing more had happened. The man charged us an astronomical daily rate. One day I figured that what we paid him was as much as if he had a full client load as a counselor every day. Several times we talked about the situation.

He skillfully sidestepped the issues. I would leave him after one or two hours, pacified, and then later realize that he had given me a lot of words but no real information. It finally reached the point where I spent much of my energies and most of my time correcting or completing the projects he had started.

"We're having serious problems," I said as I confronted him. "We need to get to the bottom of this."

"Of course, Gloria," he said.

We spent almost one whole day in mid-December in conversation. I hit him with every complaint, every frustration, every disappointment. He, like the ever-wise counselor of old, never lost his temper. Patiently and calmly he answered each question or complaint I raised.

By the end of the day, both of us were exhausted. He left me, a smile on his face, assuring me that we had gotten the problems straightened out.

The next morning he came to work. As he moved through the morning, I saw that nothing had changed. He operated as he had been during the previous weeks.

"Wait a minute," I said.

"Something wrong?" he asked.

"Wrong? I thought we had resolved everything yesterday."

"Resolved? You feel better, don't you?" he said. "Besides, things are moving along, although perhaps not as quickly as I had originally envisioned."

I closed my eyes, silently praying for wisdom before I spoke again. "I get a feeling that I wasted all day yesterday. Let's get this straight. Once and for all."

We spent almost the entire day going over the same ground we had covered the day before. By the end of the day, I felt emotionally drained and slightly frustrated. He was clever with words, always explaining theory to me when I tried to talk practical. Finally I stopped him and pinpointed the specific problem areas.

He smiled, nodded, and assured me he understood. After he left, I felt frustrated that he had taken up two full days of my time. Then I consoled myself. At least we had made progress. "Now we can get the business moving right," I said.

Had he been anyone other than the counselor B.J. and I had gone to for fifteen months, maybe I would have seen through the problem sooner. But this man had helped so much.

The third day he arrived, went into the office, and continued exactly as he had been operating since the beginning.

I wanted to scream. I couldn't believe what was happening. Fortunately B.J. had come home the night before. I ran into the bedroom and poured out the whole story of the two draining days.

"We need a man-to-man talk," B.J. said when he stepped into the office.

"Sure thing," the man answered.

For two hours they went over and over the same ground. As they talked and I mostly listened, I began to realize what was wrong.

We had learned more in the counseling situations than our psychologist realized. We had used the sessions as a time and place to work out our problems together. When problems upset us, we saved the pent-up anger and let it loose in the controlled environment of the counseling room.

Even though the counselor knew we were making progress, I don't believe that he understood how successfully we were getting our lives in focus. He had taught us well. Now we could cope without leaning on him or depending on anyone else.

In the conversation between the two men, they talked as though B.J. had never heard of procedures and systems. He explained how a system operates. "If everybody works together, the business operates like a chain. But if one link lets go, then the whole system fails."

He talked abstractions. But I needed to get the mail out!

I stood up and faced him. "You've deceived us! We have paid you a fantastic salary, and you've done nothing but cause more work for me!"

"You've been on my back every day!" For the first time he lashed back, defending himself.

I was too angry to cower. I stood my ground, and the words flew. He stormed out of our house. We never saw him again.

"We've done it again," I said to B.J. "He's done to us what all the others have done. He sabotaged our work."

"But this time," B.J. said wisely, "we caught on before he did serious damage. At least now we know what we want and we don't have to be ripped off again."

The music business can be a rip-off. You can do the things you love the most and be around exciting events and creative people. You hear top-quality entertainers. You rub shoulders with the famous and the talented.

But it also offers a place for people to grab on to you, squeeze out energy and money, never really caring about you. They come around for their own self-interests. They seem to find self-esteem just being around the glitter world.

We won't let this happen again, I promised myself.

We knew that, from here on in, we wouldn't be cheated by unqualified employees or led astray by empty promises.

26

In Tune

A few minutes after the counselor stormed out, I went to my desk. I sat down, prepared to work as usual, but I couldn't.

I thought of the overwhelming work load I faced. I started to cry and couldn't stop. I had to make choices. The choices I made meant I would do one or two things and leave a hundred others undone.

Finally, through my tears I made a decision. We had a top priority right now: a country album. We had signed the contract, and B.J. had scheduled to cut it in the studio in late December.

Some Love Songs Never Die was our first secular effort in over a year. We wanted it to be the best thing to date.

In order to get the most mileage out of that album, we had to have ourselves ready with PR, publicity, concerts, mail-outs coordinated with release dates, press events, and a lot of travel. It meant creating high exposure to the media for B.J.

We had a few musical commercials set up, which B.J. finished first, then we put our whole efforts into plugging the album when MCA released it.

But the day the counselor-turned-efficiency-expert left, I could only think of how impossible the task before me seemed. Finally, I dried my tears and started to work. It took me half an hour to get into top gear, but by lunchtime I was zooming ahead.

At that dark moment a real light had begun to shine. I didn't know it then, but we were on our way to setting up a sound business system. We would soon do an effective job of promoting B.J.

Shortly before the confrontation with the counselor I had begun interviewing for an assistant. We had put an ad in the paper and spread the word. The applicants came, and I personally interviewed each of them.

One woman stuck out. She had ambition, good references, and a dynamic personality. I was looking for a person with skills comparable to a secretary–receptionist. This tall blonde had more qualifications than I asked for. I felt she would be really unhappy with the job. I passed her over.

I couldn't remember her name (I'm terrible with names anyway), so I referred to her as "Ball of Fire."

Weeks later I had still not hired anyone and remembered "Ball of Fire." Maybe she *would* fit in, I reasoned. I remembered one thing about her—the place of her last employment. She had worked for the Southern Baptist Radio–TV Commission in Fort Worth. I called and got her name, but she had already left that position. They gave me suggestions on how I might locate her.

As if by plan, she dropped by the Southern Baptist studio one day. Someone said, "By the way, Gloria Thomas called here the other day, trying to get hold of you."

Janet Kelly (whose name I'll never forget again!) returned my call. We set up a second interview, and I hired her.

After three months on the job, Janet was progressing well, but she seemed nervous when she made mistakes. One day I realized Janet worried about being fired because of mistakes. I needed her full concentration on the job. "Janet, I want to make a pact with you. There are no mistakes bad enough that I'll fire you, if they're honest mistakes. As long as you have the business at heart, you don't need to worry about losing your job."

We shook hands. Our agreement and her commitment during those next few months carried me over rough territory.

One day I said to B.J., "If Janet's attitude could be bottled and sold, it would outsell gold."

Janet stayed beside me during long, hard hours of detailed and intricate negotiations. She never complained about extra hours or the work load. I needed that kind of committed person alongside me. It alleviated some of the stored-up pressure in me.

Aside from all the other problems, we still had a cash flow shortage that made it difficult for us. We had royalties we knew would come but we didn't have cash. And, among other things, the IRS was still on our backs.

Crash courses of rugged experience have always been my main form of education. I learned most of my lessons by reacting to crises. As I grew in my Christian experience I learned to act rather than react. I also figured out how to conduct the business end. Even though the counselor had not put in the computerized system and all the other things we had envisioned together, I had learned in the meantime.

I had to write a formal letter, for review by our attorney, to send to the ex-counselor, letting him know his relationship with us had been terminated and that he would receive no further money from us, even on the deals he had done some work on.

He had made a lot of decisions we needed to straighten out, which included work with the printers, the graphic people, and those who did the logo. We discovered that everything he had touched was in disorder.

I sat down several times to write the letter. I relived such unpleasant feelings, I wanted to run away from the whole situation. A hundred things that I needed to do popped into my mind, giving me dozens of excuses to avoid the letter. I finally realized that I was wasting energy and I needed to get the letter out. I prayed every step of the way and asked the Lord to show me how to rechannel that wasted energy.

Even so, it took me three days to complete the letter. But once it was behind me, I felt a tremendous release. Janet then took the letter and edited it. She too experienced much of the same anxiety I had felt. As she worked I saw from her face and her eyes that she suffered with me and was fatigued by the end of the day.

But once we mailed the letter we turned toward straightening out our business. I plunged into the job knowing that, with the Lord's help, I could do whatever needed to be done.

One of the few productive things that the counselor did do was to put us in touch with Jim Manley, an accountant who spent something like fifty-two straight hours putting together seven years of unkept records. At least now we had our books together enough so that we could sit down and plan a recovery strategy.

Jim, an elder in a Bible Church, is that special kind of accountant who understands numbers and deals with hard, cold logic. I've always been impressed with that quality and appreciated his grasp of facts and figures.

One day I saw a new side of Jim Manley, and God used him to make life take on a new meaning when I needed it.

We were working on the album *Amazing Grace* for Word. Everything was going wrong. Negotiations had stalled. We needed cash for an IRS payment. I just didn't know what to do. B.J. had already recorded several of the songs on tape.

I was explaining all this to Jim and put on B.J.'s tape of the songs. I left the room to get some additional material while the tape was playing.

I returned a few minutes later. And when I opened the door, Jim sat quietly on the sofa, as if glued to the spot. Tears flowed down his cheeks because B.J.'s singing touched him so deeply. "Gloria," he said, through his tears, "just play this tape."

I took his advice, played the tape for the vice-president of Word, and the negotiations moved forward again. The cash flowed.

A third member of the team was Joel Katz of Katz and Weissman, who has represented us since 1978.

Joel's a lawyer in Atlanta who already had a big list of clients like Willie Nelson, Merle Haggard, and Johnny Paycheck. He didn't need our business but accepted us as clients—maybe because we needed him so badly.

Joel has never fumbled a deal for us. He's one of the few people I'm sure I can rely on.

Once, quite soon after he became our lawyer, we talked about an upcoming project. While B.J. and I grew excited, another part of me immediately began thinking of all the problems and everything that could go wrong. I voiced several of my fears.

"Glo," Joel said quietly, "there's a time to worry, and this is not the time."

"But—but—" I stuttered.

He cupped my chin in his hands. "Don't worry until I tell you to worry. Then you can go crazy. But not until I tell you. Okay?"

I knew from then on I could count on Joel. When he says, "Don't worry," I don't. I've also learned that he never exaggerates problems or underplays them either. When Joel says, "I feel like the deal will happen," it's as good as a signed contract.

One time Joel went to Europe to represent our foreign sales. Contracts and negotiations work so differently there, and Joel found himself under extreme pressure. It affected his health and he was sick a great deal of the time.

I didn't know any of this because he never phoned or wrote us about himself or the difficulties. But while he traveled in Europe, I thought of him constantly. Not just about the business arrangements, but I felt so concerned about Joel personally. I prayed for him a dozen times a day, every day he was gone.

After he returned, we had a meeting at Loew's Anatole Hotel in Dallas. As we walked down the hallway, he mentioned the complexities of the negotiations in Europe and their physical effect on him.

"Joel," I said, "I didn't know that, but I prayed for you almost constantly every day."

He looked at me, and our eyes held for a fraction of a second. His misted up and then he turned and walked away.

It's hard to find honest and smart people in the music business. For every dollar you make, there are twelve people lined up trying to find ways to take it.

B.J. had known Pete Drake for twenty years. As the best known steel guitar player in the business, Pete had played on B.J.'s sessions back in the very early years. So when B.J. and Pete joined forces in 1981 as artist and producer to work together on a traditional hymn album, they already had mutual admiration and respect for each other's talent.

Because Pete understood how to work with B.J., respecting B.J.'s ability to make even an old song his own, but more, because of his attitude toward business and what really gives it a chance for success, Pete is not only a producer but a real friend.

At last we were beginning to find out how good life can be. We had people who worked with us as a team, and they took so much of the worry and the stress from us. We were functioning.

We had many difficulties, but they seemed so small in comparison to what we had been dealing with before.

We figured out our own system, but in early 1981 came the time to test that new system.

B.J. was out on the road, but he doesn't go alone. Nine other people travel with him, and none of them live in the same city. The entourage consists of seven band members, a road manager, and a sound man. Many times Janet and I went along. Just coordinating the flights and the equipment was almost a full-time job. That was a small part of the total work.

We also had special projects coming up. Those included television appearances, commercials, concerts, and performances at crusades. B.J. has sung for Oral Roberts, Billy Graham, Robert Schuller, and Rex Humbard.

We spent the summer of 1981 working out the problems in the system. We wanted a systematic approach so that no matter what kind of situation developed, we had provision for handling it.

Each month we average approximately a thousand letters. We feel that when people care enough to write they deserve an answer. They often request pictures or ask where they can buy a particular album or tape. We have no staff that can answer all those letters.

That's where Linda Tanis comes in. Weekly we mail the letters to her and, as president of B.J.'s fan club, she sees that they are answered—every one. Naturally there are letters we answer directly. Only recently we had one from a man ready to commit suicide and begging for help.

Linda Tanis and our fan club members have been the local folks who have helped promote B.J.'s music. We owe them more than they'll ever know.

We've come a long way, B.J. and I. We've made a lot of mistakes, but we've also had wonderful people to help make things easier for us, people like Janet, Joel, Jim, Pete, and Linda. The fan club members have been just so faithful in letting local communities know about B.J.'s appearances and urging disc jockeys to play his new releases.

Just the other day we received a wonderful letter from a person in Georgia who had been deeply touched by B.J.'s music.

"It's so rewarding, isn't it?" I said to B.J.

"Yeah," he answered. "We give ourselves to Jesus Christ, and He uses our talents to bless others."

We stood at the back door of our den, looking across our wooded yard. The evening sun glowed through the trees. I felt so close to my husband and to Jesus Christ who has given us such a rich and wonderful life together.

"Thank You, Lord," I said again and again.

B.J. has now won five Grammies—all in the inspirational category. Yet his peers don't categorize him as a gospel singer.

We believe this recognition gives him a greater sphere of influence. We discovered that only 3 percent of Christians listen to gospel radio. We want to reach a broader audience.

I feel so blessed to be part of this creative venture that God has given us.

I've also tried to write music as my creative outlet. B.J. recorded two of my songs under the Myrrh label (Word Records) for release in 1982. One of them is called "Born Again."

Stan Mosier, vice-president of Word Records heard "I Need a Miracle" and called me. "That song has potential, Gloria."

After talking it over, he pegged it for the number-two spot on the album *Miracle*. Number two meant just that—the exposure so that it could become the second release of the album.

When B.J. sings, he tries to communicate a message. He believes what he sings. If he can't feel a song's message, he won't sing it. B.J. refuses to be like a preacher who mouths theology but has no conviction about his words. The words may be right, but the sound is wrong.

As our lives grow and we find ourselves more in touch, B.J. hopes that people will catch the spirit in which he sings, even if they don't understand the words or get excited about the particular song. We want our lives to be so in tune with God that people will know there's a difference in his voice, in his style, and in his choice of music. And we also pray that they'll see Jesus Christ working in B.J.'s life.

27

Grand Ole Opry Birthday

Gloria and I are in tune now. That doesn't mean we harmonize all the time—any good instrument gets out of tune. In fact, the finer the instrument, the more sensitive it is to losing its tune.

Gloria and I stay in tune because we work at it. Our marriage works better now than before, but we know that no good marriage runs itself.

A lot of good things are going on in our lives right now. I have recently signed contracts for some of the most exciting projects of my career. We have gotten our management company, RainSong, on solid ground. We've gained the reputation of being "can-do people." Gloria is a natural at this kind of thing, and she does as well as anyone in the business.

Then, in August 1981, I reached the highlight of my career as a singer. I asked to become a member of the Grand Ole Opry. They accepted me.

I can't think of a greater honor for a singer. Being part of the Grand Ole Opry means peers in the music business recognize my contribution to music. For me, it signaled even more. The Opry had such an influence in my early life, dating back to my hearing Hank Williams when I was in third grade. This was part of my way of paying them back.

On my thirty-ninth birthday, August 7, 1981, I was inducted as the sixtieth member of the Grand Ole Opry.

Probably alongside winning a Grammy, there's no greater accolade a singer can receive. I won five Grammies, each for single performances. But for me, this membership was even greater.

What a night it was! Gloria had set up full media coverage. A wonderful group of friends celebrated the event with me. Some of the top names in the field performed for the occasion such as Jan Howard, the Gatlin Brothers, Jerry Clower, Ray Stevens, and Pete Drake.

Later we all went to the Stockyards Restaurant for an enormous press party. Gloria had arranged for representatives from all the major trade magazines to be present. Several people represented national publications. Record companies, including MCA and BMI, sent people. It was the best media-covered event I'd ever been involved in. And Gloria had been behind it all the way.

The next morning, Gloria and I sat in the airport restaurant eating breakfast. The day before I had done an interview with Ralph Emery, one of the major country disc jockeys at WSM, Nashville. The station manager, the station engineer, and Ralph Emery sat with us.

The station engineer, without realizing it, gave Gloria the greatest compliment he could. He said, "I don't know who does your PR, but this has been one of the most thoroughly covered events I have ever seen."

For Gloria, perhaps even more than for myself, it confirmed that we were now a valid company. We had our feet on solid ground. We knew what we were doing.

I smiled at the engineer and took Gloria's hand. "She's the PR."

I could tell from the response on Gloria's face that it raised her self-esteem. She had worked hard, and it had paid off. Now she knew she could do it. And I was proud of her.

As we walked to the plane together later, I had my arm lightly around her waist. I felt very close to my wife. Close, not just because we are husband and wife. But close because we're partners and we have a good life together. We're growing as two separate people and, at the same time, growing together as one. We think that's God's plan for us.

We're learning, every day, just how good life can be.